Igor Nemtsev

The Elshad System
For White

MONGOOSE
Press

BOSTON

Publisher: Mongoose Press
1005 Boylston Street, Suite 324
Newton Highlands, MA 02461
info@mongoosepress.com
www.MongoosePress.com

ISBN: 978-1-936277-92-6

Distributed to the trade by National Book Network
custserv@nbnbooks.com, 800-462-6420
For all other sales inquiries please contact the Publisher.

Layout: Stanislav Makarov
Editor: Jorge Amador
Translator: Jim Marfia
Cover Design: Alexander Krivenda
Printed in the United States of America

First English edition
0 9 8 7 6 5 4 3 2 1

Contents

Foreword

Dear Reader,

I am very happy that you have purchased my book; but you, too, have reason to be happy. Those of you who a year ago purchased the first book on the Elshad System have asked me many times whether one may also play this system with White? The answer is: Yes!

Indeed, the inventor of this system, Elshad Mamedov, did so himself. He started using his system way back in 1975. The universality of the system is such that it can be played, not only as Black, but also as White. Having absorbed the basic setups and piece maneuvers, you may use Elshad's Opening against any opposition.

The system works especially well in blitz and rapid games. Why? Very simple: a player who has never before encountered this opening, starts eating up his time because he doesn't understand how to react to it. Is it possible realistically to expect him to do this in a three-minute game? This turns out to be one of our main assets. And fighting psychology is no less important. Our opponent, facing "this trash," gets nervous; if you're playing the game in the park, they might even say something right to your face. They'll consider it necessary to refute this sort of thing and overpress.

In this book, we have presented some of Elshad's games, some of mine, and some by other chessplayers – including a future grandmaster, Vasily Papin. The opening's philosophy is laid out in the Introduction. I have to say: the popularity of Elshad's Opening is enormous! I have even managed to play, over the Internet, a thematic match against FIDE Master Konstantin Kozlov – which I won 5.5-4.5. Thus did I defend this opening's honor!

Discover for yourself this new chess frontier!

Introduction

1.c3

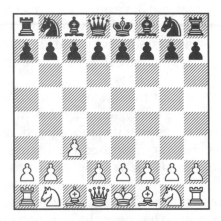

And so, we begin. Naturally, the first time you see this kind of opening move, various feelings begin to come over you: confusion, contempt – anger, even. How can he play such nonsense – and against *me?* Does he think I'm some sort of patzer?

However, strictly speaking, what has happened here? White has simply *declined to advance* his center pawn two spaces as classical theory teaches. Does this mean, then, that he has played an "incorrect" opening move? Not at all. I would agree with those who say that White has forfeited his first-move advantage: so be it. Now Black is offered the opportunity to occupy the center with his own pawn – to move "first," as it were. Is he ready for this? I don't think so. In fact, what's the idea behind having the first move? We have opened a path to the queenside for the queen – and to what end? Slow down; all will be revealed in due course. Every move in Elshad's Opening will be explained, one at a time.

But really, what is Black to do now? The replies 1...e5 or 1...d5 seem logical now. Also, 1...♘f6 or 1...c5 are sometimes played here. For now, we'll take these in order:

1...d5

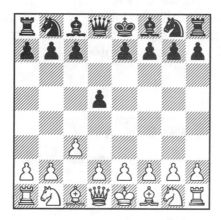

By far the most natural response. Why? Well, if only because 1.c3 would make it a Closed Game. Also, because not everyone would respond to 1.e4 with 1...e5. Of course, now Black would clearly want to set another pawn up in the center next move. We have no objection to this.

1) 1...e5:

Certainly, this is an excellent opening move. White keeps playing his game. First, he brings the queen out to the fourth rank.

2.♕a4 (hah! – Black is prevented from following up with 2...d5 right away) 2...♞f6. Naturally. Now White is at a crossroads: he could play 3.e4, which sometimes brings positions reminiscent of Ponziani's Opening; however, Elshad's concept sets out something completely different in this variation. We might continue his plan of preparing h2-h3 and g2-g4, with a kingside attack. Each of these approaches will have its own chapter.

2) 1...♘f6:

A universal reply. Black waits to see what his opponent does. Will he go back to theoretical lines? No!

2.♕a4 g6

Setting up a nice, safe house for the king – anyway, that's what it looks like for Black.

3.d3 ♗g7 4.g4

Still not looking too dangerous.

4...0-0 5.g5 ♘d5 6.♗g2 ♘b6 7.♕f4

Not to h4 right away. First we must let the pawn move forward.

7...♘c6 8.h4 d5 9.h5 e5 10.♕h4, and we are back on the main road. In a practical game, the threat of h5xg6 is unstoppable.

3) 1...c5:

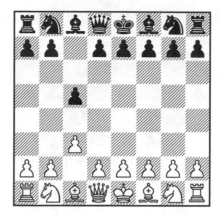

Welcome to the strategic department in the Elshad. In this variation, Black occupies way too much space.

2.d3

Humble. Of course, White could (and should) also play ♕d1-a4.

2...d5 3.♘d2 e5 4.h3 f5 5.g4:

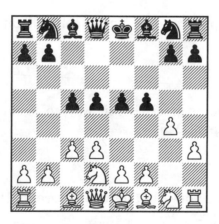

There's a novelty for you! Isn't the pawn hanging? Why not take it? Undoubtedly, that's what Black is thinking. Meanwhile, time is rushing past, especially when you're playing on the Internet at three minutes a game, with no increment.

5...fxg4 6.hxg4 ♗xg4 7.♗g2 ♘f6 8.♘f1 ♘c6 9.♘e3:

Some of White's ideas start to emerge. The d5-pawn is clearly weak. It may also be attacked by the white queen from b3. And Black certainly doesn't want to cede the light-squared bishop, because those squares around his king would be decisively weakened.

9...♗e6

Everything appears to be under control! But Black is sadly mistaken!

10.♘h3

The knight moves precisely this way, so as not to block his g2-bishop. The threat is ♘g5.

10...h6

Black feels safe now – but only for a second. He thinks that he has prevented ♘g5.

11.♘g5

And here's Elshad's Surprise!

11...♕d7 (of course, not 11...hxg5 12.♖xh8) 12.♘xe6 ♕xe6 13.♕b3.

The d5-pawn is now attacked three times. Many players now commit the decisive error of... castling.

13...0-0-0 14.♗h3:

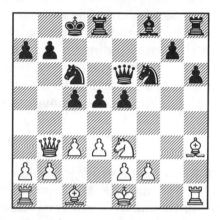

And the queen drops: *la commedia è finita!* How can one lose a game in just fifteen moves, after making nothing but good progress? The answer is that, in the opening, we need to play concretely. But how do we do this while the clock is ticking? When we have but three minutes for the entire game? Well, let our opponents think about that; whereas in this book, I give White a full guide to navigating through the ideas. In certain circumstances, you will manage to beat whomever you like. Grandmasters, even.

2.♕a4+

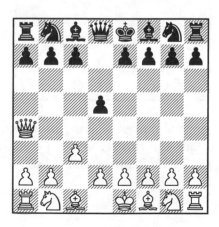

Your basic move in this opening. It looks like pure ineptness: an early queen move instead of a "classical" occupation of the center with pawns, or bringing out the minor pieces first. What does White achieve by this? You can be almost one hundred percent certain that your opponent is seeing this position for the first time in his life. Thinking himself "disrespected," he will want to punish you for such play. He'll start thinking, and thinking, and thinking how to do it – all the while with his time winding down in blitz or rapid chess. Even in a game with a classical time control, though, a refutation does not seem possible. Yes, according to theory, Black shouldn't have any problems, but in practice he'll have quite a few of them.

So we have brought our queen out to a4. Why? It couldn't be just to give check... Well, of course not. Our queen plans to redeploy in short order to the king's wing. It would be especially good for it to end up at h4, but only after the h-pawn reaches h5. So we avoid blocking the fourth rank with pawns or pieces. Our opponent doesn't know this; and he usually brings his pieces out simply and normally, to their typical squares.

2...c6

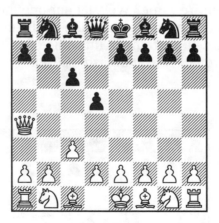

One of several normal moves. Having buttressed the d5-pawn, Black can bravely face the future. Other possible moves in this position are 2...♘c6, 2...♘d7, and even 2...♗d7.

2...♘c6:

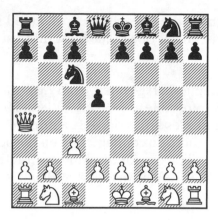

It is most natural to develop the knight. But in this line, Black defends his d5-pawn insecurely.

3.d3

Creating a corridor for the b1-knight to go through d2 and on to f1. Now, why does it want to go to f1? Hold on a bit, this will soon become clear.

3...e5

All according to plan. If your opponent lets you, you should occupy the center with pawns.

4.h3

Few would believe at this stage that this move will serve as an escape square down the line. What is clear is that White is preparing to play g2-g4.

4...♘f6

Contrary to White's play, Black does not intend to refrain from normal piece development.

Instead, Black may try 4...f5, apparently preventing White from playing g2-g4. But no, that's exactly what we're going to play: 5.g4!.

In fact, even without the queen on a4, we could still play g2-g4, sacrificing a pawn. This is one of the most interesting twists of the Elshad Opening.

Play might continue 5...fxg4 6.hxg4 ♘f6 7.g5 (the black pieces are feeling most uncomfortable) 7...♘d7 8.♗g2 ♘b6 9.♕h4. The white queen arrives on Black's kingside. Just a minute ago, things were OK for Black; now, there's a conflagration on the board. There is no guidepost in classical theory for this kind of situation. What to do? How do I play this? Time's a-wastin', and Black is getting nervous.

5.g4

The pawn is prepared to go still further, to g5. When that happens, keep in mind that the white bishop will soon come out to g2, keeping a constant watch on the d5-pawn .

5...h6

Well, that does it: Black can breathe freely now. For the time being, the threat of g4-g5 is prevented. And now, it looks like he can prepare to castle. But Black still doesn't know that the h6-pawn will soon become a major problem. It's precisely that pawn that will become the focus of White's attack.

6.♗g2 ♗e7 7.♘d2 0-0

It's pretty much all over; Black has fallen. Formally, everything appears to be in order, he's still breathing. But no human could possibly make 15 consecutive best moves. We are playing against humans and so we will focus our attack on them.

8.♘f1

The knight goes to g3. Why? It's all very simple: the black monarch has already castled on the kingside. There is no longer any point in bringing the knight to e3 when we can carry out a direct attack on the king. From the g3 square, the knight will aim at the vital squares f5 and h5. And we're going to batter down his castled position with g4-g5.

3.d3

To control the fourth rank, and to facilitate the transfer of the knight to f1 via d2.

3...♘f6 4.h3 g6

One of Black's possible ways to develop. It looks quite secure.

5.g4 ♗g7 6.♗g2 0-0 7.g5

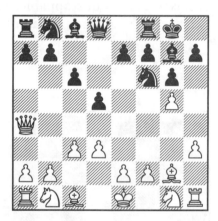

Here's yet another important crossroads. Which way will the knight go?

7...♘h5

A quick reaction; this is quite often the way it's played. But Black remains unaware of White's vital threat.

7...♘fd7 is possible, but then White carries out a direct storm with his h-pawn, for example 8.h4 e5 9.h5 ♘c5 10.♕h4:

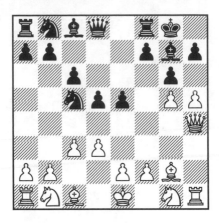

The culmination! White has fully carried out his opening intentions. The threat of h5xg6 is now unstoppable. You can see how to play the attack correctly from this position by analyzing the appropriate games.

8.♗f3

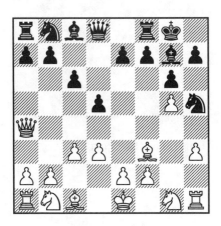

Here it is!! Black's knight has nowhere to retreat, and White will play ♗xh5. Next the queen goes to h4, and White's knight enters via b1-d2-f1-g3-h5.

8...c5 9.♗xh5 gxh5 10.♕h4 ♗f5 11.♘d2 ♗g6 12.♘f1 ♘d7 13.♘g3 ♖e8 14.♘xh5

There will be games along these lines in this book.

Chapter 1

//

Black Plays ...d7-d5, Thinking "Closed Game"

1. nemtsevguru (2405) – durdevic (2253)

lichess.org, 2 November 2017

1.c3 d5 2.♕a4+ c6

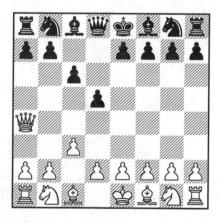

One of Black's best approaches to the Elshad Opening in this position – especially when considering that White plans to play g2-g4 and then develop his light-squared bishop to g2. Black would like to construct what is known in Russia as the "panzer" formation *[named after German tanks – Ed.]*, consisting of pawns at c6, d5, and e5.

3.h3

One might also play g2-g4! at once. The text move is a little more subtle. At the moment, Black is clearly thinking that he's playing a "fool," or else a drunkard if the game is on the Internet. Because understanding, on the fly, what's on White's mind would be impossible. And what, indeed, is White up to? White is developing the pieces according to the Elshad scheme, and is awaiting Black's kingside castling – at which point the g-pawn will be set loose to assault Black's castled position and the queen will unexpectedly (for Black) leap from the a4 square to the kingside. To h4!

3...♘f6

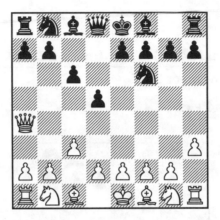

Here White could still be clever with d2-d3.

4.g4 h6

A standard reaction to White's last move; however, it has a flaw. If Black now castles short, then the h6-pawn will become a clear target for a White attack with g4-g5!

5.♗g2 e5

It's hard to imagine a more natural move.

6.d3

Not just developing, but also an important bit of strategic accuracy. White prepares to bring the knight out to d2. And – this is important! – if Black crosses the line of demarcation now with ...e5-e4, then White can take with d3xe4!

6...♗d6 7.♘d2

The knight is following Elshad's path.

7...♗d7

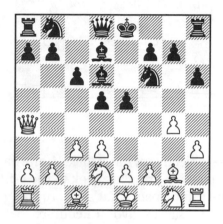

8.♘f1!

That's the spot! Black has just placed his bishop on d7 – is it possible that he plans to continue ...c6-c5 ? This would drive White's queen back to b3 or c2. But the important thing is that the d5-pawn would thus be weakened. White could then play his knight to e3, inducing ...d5-d4, and returning at once to f1 to come out to g3 and then to e4!

8...0-0

8...c5 9.♕c2! (or 9.♕b3 ♗c6 10.♘e3 d4 11.♗xc6+ ♘xc6 12.♕xb7 ♖c8 13.♘c4) 9...0-0 10.♘e3 d4 11.♘f1 ♘c6 12.♘g3 ♖c8 13.♘f3 b5 14.♘h4 a6 15.♘gf5 ♗xf5 16.♘xf5 ♖e8 17.g5! hxg5 18.♗xg5, and White is on the attack. Although the engines may disapprove of White's concept, in fact this is nothing new. On the other hand, here *Stockfish* 8 will not give White even a small advantage!

9.♘g3 ♘a6

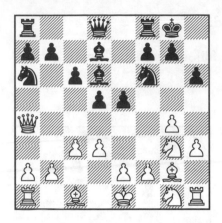

10.g5

This is the chief objective of the attack. White has no intention of castling here: he plans to bring his rook to the g-file, which means he should pry the g-file open. That's where that pawn's being on h6 comes in – not in Black's favor, of course.

10.e4!? is another possibility in these positions. Elshad himself has played this not infrequently. I myself haven't grown to the point of such advanced piloting! The game might continue 10...dxe4 11.dxe4 ♞c5 12.♕c2 ♕c7 13.♞1e2 ♝e6 14.♞f5, with an attack.

10...hxg5 11.♝xg5 ♝e7 12.♞f3?!

However, this is an inaccuracy, since after ...e5-e4 the queen might not get to the kingside (12.♕h4!).

12...♕c7

12...e4!? 13.dxe4! (White must capture) 13...dxe4 14.♝xf6 ♞c5 15.♝xe7 ♕xe7 16.♕d4 exf3 17.♝xf3 ♜fe8 18.h4±. Who understands what's going on, over the board? *Stockfish* 8 gives White a large advantage, and I agree.

13.♕h4 ♝e6

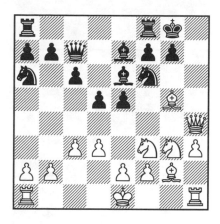

14.♖g1

Nimzowitsch would have been satisfied with this mysterious rook move – mysterious for Black, that is, not for White. Those who have my book on the Elshad System for Black will know that this rook will soon participate in checkmating the enemy king.

14.d4!? very much deserves attention: 14...e4 15.♘e5 ♖fe8 16.f3! exf3 17.♗xf3 c5 (Black is trying to strike a blow in the center, just as "the book" says) 18.♖g1± cxd4 19.♘f5 ♕xe5 20.♘xg7 ♔xg7 21.♗xf6+ ♔f8 22.♕h8#:

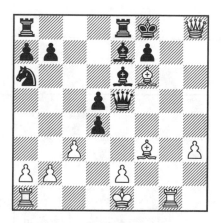

14...♕b6 15.0-0-0 ♕a5 16.♔b1 d4 17.c4

And let's not overlook the capture on a2...

17...b5

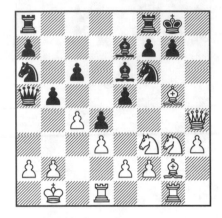

18.♘xe5!

A vitally important attacking principle for opposite-side castling: "firstest with the mostest!"

18...bxc4 19.♘xc6

Fork.

19...♕c7 20.♘xe7+ ♕xe7 21.♗xa8 ♖xa8 22.♘h5 cxd3 23.♘xf6+ ♔f8

23...gxf6 24.♗xf6+ ♔f8 25.♕h8#.

24.♕h8#

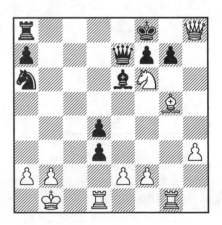

2. nemtsevguru (2412) – jac39 (2303)

lichess.org, 2 November 2017

1.c3 d5 2.♕a4+ ♗d7

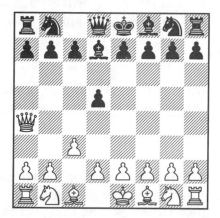

A fairly common continuation. But it does have a considerable drawback: the bishop is like a log that has fallen in the middle of the road. Trying to bring it out later to c6 only aggravates the problem: where do you put the queen's knight?

3.♕b3

Now there are two pawns under attack, on b7 and d5. There follows the standard reaction to White's last move:

3...♗c6

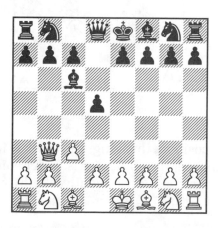

4.d4

Here I employed an old recommendation by Valery Chashchikhin in his pamphlet on the Elshad System for Black. On c6, the bishop reminds me of a big brother to Black's pawns at d5 and b7: it holds their hands, as if all three of them were walking somewhere together...

4...♘d7 5.♘f3

Now the pawn structure itself is telling me how my pieces should be developed: in the spirit of the London System.

5...♘gf6 6.♗f4 g6 7.e3 ♗g7 8.♗d3

This is the most accurate. The development of the queen's knight can wait a bit. We might see a transformation into a hybrid of the Chigorin and Grünfeld Defenses. And then, perhaps, White might have to reorder his game on the queenside with c3-c4 – perhaps allowing the knight, now on b1, to come out to c3!

8...0-0

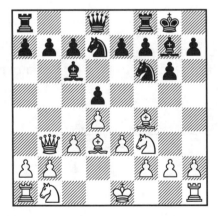

9.h4

In the current position, this kingside attack is justified because the center is stabilized, the e5 square is under control, and White has not castled kingside. Consequently, the h1-rook, like a gun, shoots the h-pawn to h5!

9...♘e4 10.♘bd2 ♘df6 11.♘e5

The immediate capture 11.♗xe4!? dxe4 12.♘e5 was worth looking into: it would have given Black problems all over the board.

11...♖b8

Black passes up the opportunity to "deprive" White's king of castling, since obviously White's king would be ideally placed on d2, letting the queen's rook through to join the kingside attack! Here is a rough variation – not forced, certainly, but showing what a typical attack in this kind of position might go like. In contrast to similar variations from the Sicilian Defense (e.g., the Dragon Variation) or the King's Indian, White attacks while Black has no targets for counterattack: 11...♘xd2 12.♔xd2 h5 13.g4 hxg4 14.♖ag1 a5 15.h5 ♘xh5 16.♖xg4 ♘xf4 17.exf4 a4 18.♕c2 ♕d6 19.♗xg6 fxg6 20.♖xg6 e6 21.♖xg7+ ♔xg7 22.♕g6#.

12.♘xe4 ♘xe4 13.♗xe4 dxe4

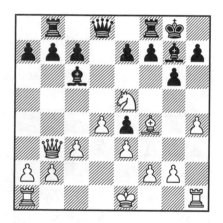

14.h5!

The positional course, capturing on c6, was also worth looking into: 14.♘xc6!? bxc6 15.♕a3 e5 16.♗g3 exd4 17.cxd4 ♕d5 18.0-0 a5 19.♖fc1, and Black's position is coming apart at the seams, as classic chess annotators might put it.

14...♗d5

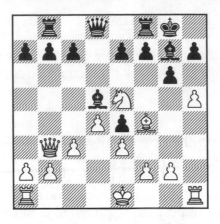

14...♗xe5 looks quite risky. It weakens the king, especially the dark squares around it. White's advantage keeps growing, as the following variation given below demonstrates (although, on the other hand, non-standard positions require non-standard solutions): 15.♗xe5 g5 16.h6 ♕d7 17.♗g7 ♖fd8 18.a4 ♕d5 19.c4 ♕a5+ 20.♔e2 a6 21.d5 ♗d7 22.♗d4±.

15.♕d1

A lost opportunity: 15.c4!. This would have been a most appealing move, leading to a powerful attack. Behold this sequence: 15...♗e6 16.d5 ♗f5 17.hxg6 hxg6 18.g4 ♗xe5 19.♗xe5 ♗xg4 20.♖h8#.

15...b5 16.♕g4 c5 17.hxg6 fxg6

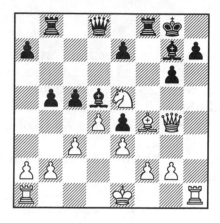

18.♘xg6?!

The twists and turns of blitz! This apparently "winning" continuation leads only to an attack that leaves White with some advantage. Meanwhile, 18.♕h4! was simple and decisive. The threat is mate on h7, and there is no defense. Here's a sample variation: 18...h5 19.♘xg6 ♖xf4 20.♘xe7+ ♔f8 21.♕xf4+ ♔xe7 22.♖xh5 ♗e6 23.♖h7 ♕g8 24.♕c7+ ♔f6 25.♖xg7 ♕xg7 26.♕xb8.

18...hxg6 19.♕xg6

19.♗xb8!?. This decision was difficult to foresee, but it is what White should have played! It looked to me as though the bishop might still prove useful for my attack on the king: 19...♕xb8 20.♕xg6 ♖f7 21.♕h7+ ♔f8 22.♕h8+ ♗xh8 23.♖xh8+ ♔g7 24.♖xb8.

19...♖f6 20.♕h7+ ♔f8

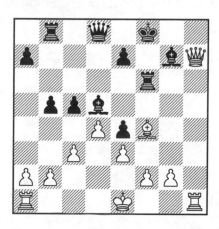

21.♗e5

21.dxc5!? was one more missed opportunity. The variation, though long, was nearly forced – and very convincing: 21...♗g8 22.♕xe4 ♖c8 23.♗e5 ♖f7 24.♖d1 ♕e8 25.♖d5 a6 26.♗xg7+ ♖xg7 27.♖f5+ ♗f7 28.♖h8+ ♖g8 29.♖h7 ♖g7 30.♖h6 ♖d8 31.♕f4 e6 32.♖h8+ ♔e7 33.♖xe8+ ♗xe8 34.♕c7+ ♖d7 35.♕e5 ♖g6 36.c6+−.

21...♗g8 22.♕xe4 ♖bb6 23.♗xf6 ♖xf6 24.dxc5 ♖e6 25.♕f3+ ♖f6 26.♕e2 ♗c4

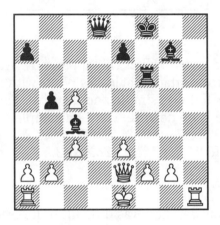

27.♕d2?

A mistake; I didn't notice that Black could simply take the queen, then the rook takes on f2. I think that, at this point, we were both playing with just seconds left. So please don't judge us too harshly.

27.♕g4± ♕d3 28.♖d1 ♕g6 29.♕xg6 ♖xg6 30.♖d8+ ♔f7 31.♖5 a6 32.a3 e5 33.♖a8. This variation shows how I should have played: rook and 4 pawns are clearly stronger than the bishop pair.

27...♕a8 28.0-0-0 ♕xg2 29.♕d8+ ♔f7 30.♖hg1 ♕xf2

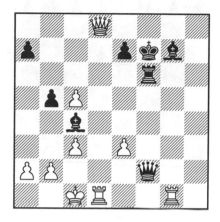

31.♖xg7+

A nice finish. When you're playing blitz, and there's only seconds left for both of you, with Black having "this kind of king," clearly the game will not continue for long.

31...♔xg7 32.♕xe7+ ♔g6 33.♕e4+ ♔g5 34.♕e5+ ♖f5

34...♕f5 35.♖g1+ ♔h6 36.♕h2+ ♕h5 37.♕b8 ♔h7 38.♕b7+ ♕f7 39.♕h1+ ♖h6 40.♕e4+ ♖g6 41.c6±.

35.♕g7+

There is no defense against the rook check along the h-file. **1-0**

3. Nemtsev_Igor (2828) – lefik-kb (2569)

05 July 2015

1.d3 d5 2.c3 e5

You can also open the game with 1.d3. This will cause a "chain reaction" of moves by Black – as in this game, where the second player simply occupies the center himself. This is just what we need. After all, in some closed openings it's possible for our opponent to play (for example) 1.d4 ♘f6, not seizing the center with pawns. But this would be bad for me here. How so? What should I play against this, he thinks. And he'll feel obligated to punish White's passive play. But indeed, what has happened in the first couple of moves? White has failed to occupy the center with his pawns. Now, does this mean that it's all over and White loses?! Not at all! White may have frittered away his assigned small opening advantage. Let's say that the game is equal... but not more than that! Black is constantly falling into this psychological trap.

3.♘d2 ♘f6 4.h3

You may also play the Elshad System without the queen sortie to a4. You should play it different ways, so that they'll have a harder time preparing for you.

4...♗e7 5.g4!

Not just in preparation for the kingside attack, but also an important positional move: it threatens the d-pawn! Let's say that, with the bishop already on g2, g2-g4 has been played. Often, Black's knight develops to d7, when suddenly– the d-pawn falls!

5...c6

A typical choice for Black – and a good one. However, let's examine Black's pieces. The f6-knight stands poorly, since it must always be on the lookout for g4-g5. It would be far better for this knight to be on e7, so that it could come out to g6 and, from there, to f4 or h4.

6.♗g2 ♘bd7

Black clearly is afraid to castle short – and not without reason.

7.♘f1

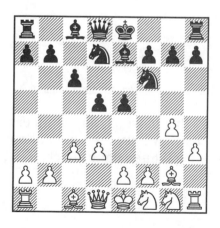

The famous Elshad knight's journey! The idea is to bring this knight to e3 or g3. In this case, it would be better to bring it to g3. Why? Well, let's say that, after Black castles, the g4-g5 push becomes quite strong: where does the knight go from f6? The h5 square will be under the control of White's g3-knight. The knight would go to e3 in order to attack the d5-pawn one more time; but in this case that is well defended by the pawn on c6. So that means that we can arrive at an important strategic conclusion: when Black's pawn stands on c5, one must bring the knight to e3!, inducing the d-pawn to advance to d4. At this point, the knight drops back to f1!!, when the diagonal for the fianchettoed king's bishop has come open; and from f1 the knight will come out, first to g3, and then to e4!

7...♘c5

7...c5? 8.g5 ♘g8 9.♗xd5±; 7...h6 8.♕c2 c5 9.♘e3 d4 10.♘f1 0-0 11.♘g3 ♖e8 12.♘f5! (12.♘e4!).

8.♘g3 ♕c7 9.♕c2!

The idea behind this move is very simple: to control the e4 square! Obviously Black will try for a breakthrough in the center, thematically answering White's flank attack. Here, White is already preparing to meet it.

9...♗e6 10.♘f3

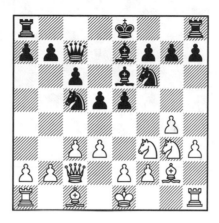

Every time Black brings out his bishop to e6, immediately we bring our knight out to f3; this is so that, when we get the chance, we can shoot our knight out to g5. Sometimes Black reflexively continues ...h7-h6 here, to prevent ♘f3-g5. But ...h7-h6 creates a target for attack on the black king, once he castles short.

10...e4 11.dxe4

The standard choice: we will always take the black pawn on e4 or c4 as soon as it gets there.

11.♘d4!? exd3 12.exd3 is worth looking into: 12...g6 13.b4 ♘cd7 14.0-0 0-0 15.♗h6 ♖fe8 16.g5 ♘h5 17.♘xh5 gxh5 18.f4±.

11...♘cxe4 12.♘xe4 ♘xe4 13.♘d4 ♘c5 14.♘xe6 ♘xe6

14...fxe6 15.0-0 0-0 16.e4 ♘d7 17.f4 doesn't change things.

15.a4 ♛e5

16.f4?!

I must admit that I am not proud of some of the moves I made around here: they could have resulted in a lost game for me. Yet here's the paradox: these games were played on the Internet, at three minutes per side. My opponent couldn't see me. The idea was, he wasn't supposed to fall for any psychological tricks – but he did! It's strange, but in such circumstances they usually reply quickly, just like my opponent. Here I attacked – and he moved away. Blitz magic!

16...♕c7

16...♘xf4 17.♗xf4 ♕xf4.

17.f5?

17.0-0! 0-0 18.e4 dxe4 19.♗xe4 h6 20.♗e3 ♖ad8 21.♕f2, with counterplay.

17...♘c5

17...♕g3+ 18.♔f1 ♗h4−+.

18.b4 ♘d7 19.a5 ♘e5 20.0-0

Finally the sequence has ended. As you can see, Black all along could have brought his queen into g3, which would have finished me off.

20...♘c4 21.e4 0-0 22.exd5 cxd5

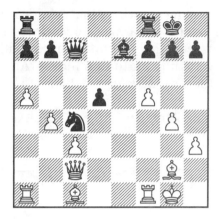

23.f6!?

23.g5!?. This way of conducting the attack is quite instructive: analyze in detail the variation I am about to present. You should learn this attacking method – it's magical!

23...♗d6 24.♗xd5 ♖ad8 25.♕e4 ♘e5 26.♗d2 ♖fe8 27.♖ae1 ♗c5+ 28.♔g2 ♕d7 29.c4 ♗f8:

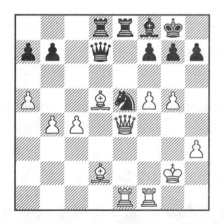

30.g6 ♘xg6 31.fxg6 ♖xe4 32.♖xe4+− ♕d6 33.gxf7+ ♔h8 34.♖f2 ♕g6+ 35.♖g4 ♕d6 36.♖e2 ♕d7 37.♖ge4 h6 38.♖e8 ♔h7 39.♖2e6 g6 40.♗e3 ♗xb4 41.♖g8 ♖xg8 42.fxg8♕+ ♔xg8 43.♖d6+ ♕f7 44.♖d8+ ♗f8 45.♗xf7+ ♔xf7 46.♖d7+ ♔e6 47.♖xb7+−.

23...♗xf6 24.♖xf6

This was the exchange sacrifice that my idea consisted of. The engine considers that the advantage now belongs to Black, but this is a mirage. In blitz, especially in unfamiliar situations, facing who knows what, it's very difficult to find moves. And with only three minutes to think, there's practically no chance to fend off this attack.

24...gxf6 25.♗h6 ♖fe8 26.♕f5 ♕e5 27.♗xd5 ♘d6 28.♕xe5 fxe5

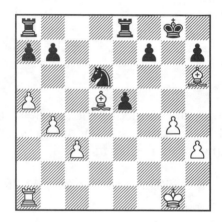

29.c4

I had seen 29.a6!±; but, heeding the advice of "the classics" for blitz – and above all, that of Genrikh Chepukaitis – I simply kept to my original plan. If you try thinking up something new with every move, then of course three minutes won't be enough for you. White is winning after 29...♖ab8 30.axb7 ♘xb7 31.c4 ♘d6 32.♖xa7 ♖xb4 33.♖d7.

29...♖e7 30.♖f1 ♖d8 31.♖f6

31.♗g5 wins more quickly: 31...♖dd7 32.♗xe7 ♖xe7 33.♔f2 ♔g7 34.♔e3 f6 35.a6 bxa6 36.♖a1+−.

31...♘e8 32.♖f5 ♖c7 33.♖g5+ ♔h8 34.♖xe5 f6 35.♖e6 b6 36.a6

36.axb6. Yes, this would have been stronger than the move I played: 36...axb6 37.♖xb6+−.

36...♖cd7 37.b5 ♖d6 38.♖e7 ♖6d7 39.♖e3 ♘d6 40.♖f3 ♘e8 41.♔g2 ♖xd5

What else to do?

42.cxd5 ♖xd5

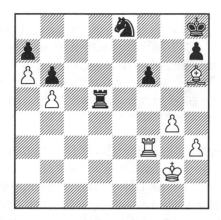

43.♖e3!

The rook goes for the seventh rank! Now it's all over.

43...♖d8 44.♖e7 ♘d6 45.♖xa7 ♘xb5 46.♖b7 ♘d4 47.♗g7+ ♔g8 48.♗xf6 ♘e6 49.♗xd8 ♘xd8 50.♖b8 ♔f7 51.♖xd8 1-0

4. Elshad – Zakurdyayeva

20 May 2015

1.c3 d5 2.♕a4+ ♘c6 3.g4

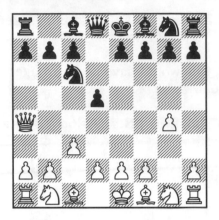

3...♗d7

This is not what you would call a "strong" move. I'm going to tell you a secret: when Black (or White) plays like this in some openings, he holds a secret thought that, "he's played an early queen sortie, so I'm going to punish him for it." How quickly we leap to conclusions! The problem is, the knight has no good jumps. This whole construction is artificial-looking. Our queen is not afraid of it. Black's pieces are crowded; his bishop hinders his queen. And one has to admit that, on a "micro" level, the d5-pawn is protected by the queen. Now it's going to always be under constant scrutiny by White's pieces. In addition, I advise you to pay attention to the b7- and d5-pawns, and along with them the c6-knight. This is a rather clumsy setup, with the knight not protecting them. It stands nearby, but does not protect. The light-squared bishop standing at g2 will clearly be overjoyed at such a prospect.

4.♗g2 ♘e5?!

And here come the consequences. Having said "A," we must also say "B." We are breaking the rules of the opening – among others, the one that says, "don't move the same piece twice in the opening." On the other hand, in Elshad's Opening, there is a lot of strangeness, and a lot of rules broken.

5.♕b3

The standard solution: the queen goes to b3, attacking Black's weakened pawns. But there is also another solution: 5.♕d4!?, for example 5...♘g6 6.♕xd5 c6 7.♕b3 ♗xg4? (Black need only stumble for a second, and immediately there comes the punishment) 8.♕xb7 ♖c8 9.♗xc6+ ♗d7 10.♕xd7+ ♕xd7 11.♗xd7+ ♔xd7 12.d3+−:

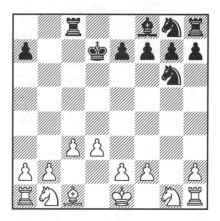

White simply has two extra pawns, plus a totally winning position.

5...e6

5...♘xg4 is possible but risky; the variations just illustrate what might happen. In a lot of cases, I am deliberately not showing Black's best moves. First of all, I want to let the reader find them on his own; and second − I want to show off some beautiful ideas!

6.♗xd5 ♗c6 (6...e6 7.♗f3 ♘e5 8.♕xb7 ♖b8 9.♕xa7 ♘xf3+ 10.♘xf3±) 7.♗xf7+ ♔d7 8.♕e6#:

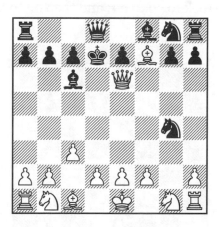

6.h3 c5 7.d3 ♗d6 8.♘d2 ♘e7 9.♕c2

9.c4!?. Counterattacking with the pawns is also very plausible, since Black doesn't have a c6-pawn to protect it. Breaking up the diagonal would be positionally well justified. Play might continue 9...0-0 10.♘gf3 ♘xf3+ 11.♘xf3 ♗c6 12.h4 d4 13.h5.

9...♗c6 10.a4

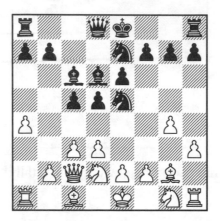

This move needs to be discussed in some depth. Considering that White is attacking on the kingside, what's the purpose of opening a second front? The point is that, as Black's king has still not castled, White is going to demonstrate that a warm welcome awaits him no matter where the monarch settles. In addition, the a-pawn is a battering ram, and messes with Black's psychology, distracting her (if only a little). In some variations, by pushing on to a5, it opens up a path for the a1-rook to go to a4, and then on to the king's wing.

10...0-0

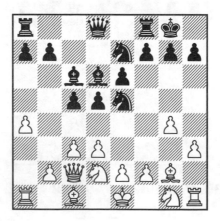

Now that Black has given up and castled, we shall proceed with our kingside attack.

11.g5 d4

Strictly speaking, this is correct. Black simply must seek some breakthrough. On the other hand, the vital square e4 is now completely in White's hands.

12.♘e4

12.♗xc6!? would have been even better: 12...♘7xc6 13.♘e4 ♗e7 14.h4 g6 15.h5 ♖c8 16.f4 ♘g4 17.♘f3±. Notice the knight on e4 and then the pawn on g5, which is guaranteeing the knight its perpetual post!

12...♘f5 13.h4 ♘g4 14.h5 h6

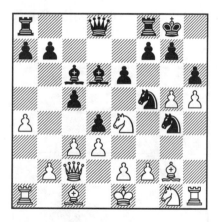

Extremely risky. Moving pawns in front of your king is a sin: everybody knows that.

15.a5

Black's head is spinning! She awaits an attack on her king, while greetings arrive on the other wing!

15...♗e7 16.♘f3

16.♗f3!? would be a worthy alternative to the text move: 16...♘e5 17.gxh6 ♘xf3+ 18.♘xf3 ♘h6 19.♖g1 ♔h8 20.♗xh6 gxh6 21.♕d2±:

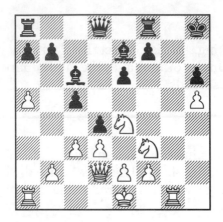

And, really, that's all there is to it.

16...hxg5 17.a6 ♕c7 18.♘fxg5 ♗xg5 19.axb7 ♗xb7 20.♗xg5 ♘xf2

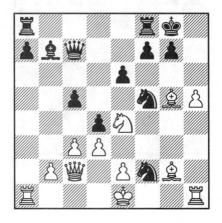

20...f6!.

21.♖g1!!

There are some boring people who, armed with silicon machinery, would like to affix a pair of question marks to this move. But I do this – for Beauty! An unbelievably mysterious move by the rook! Nimzowitsch would have been delighted. Have you seen how Black gets mated on the g-file? Yes, there was a refutation... but I'm not going to show it to you!

21.♔xf2! (this would also be a worthy solution to this position) 21...♗xe4 22.dxe4 ♕g3+ 23.♔g1 ♘e3 24.♗xe3 ♕xe3+ 25.♔f1±, when White has an extra piece and every prospect of winning.

21...♗xe4 22.♗xe4 ♘h3 23.0-0-0 ♘xg5 24.♗xf5

24.♖xg5!?. Keep an eye on this variation: 24. ♕f4+ 25.♕d2 ♕xd2+ 26.♔xd2 f6 27.♖xf5 exf5 28.♗xa8 ♖xa8 29.♖f1 ♖b8 30.♔c2 ♔f7 31.♖xf5±. In this rook ending, White keeps a stable advantage due to his more active rook and more compact pawn mass.

24...exf5 25.♖xg5 dxc3 26.♕xc3 ♕f4+ 27.♕d2 ♕e5

27...♕xd2+ (this of course would have been the proper line for Black) 28.♔xd2 ♖ab8 29.♔c3 ♖b4 30.♖dg1 ♖g4 31.♖1xg4 fxg4 32.e4 ♖b8 33.♖xg4±:

28.♖dg1

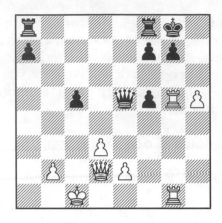

28...g6 29.hxg6 fxg6 30.♖xg6+ ♔f7 31.♕h6 ♖ab8 32.♖g7+ ♔e8 33.♕c6+ ♔d8 34.♕d7# 1-0

5. Nemtsev_Igor (2843) – Anton_Shamnae (2329)

5 July 2015

1.c3 d5 2.♕a4+ c6 3.g4 e6

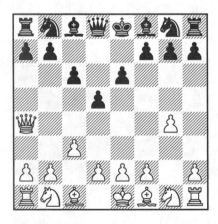

The Elshad versus the triangle. Nowadays, I think that here, moving the bishop to g2 is not so necessary. It would be more interesting to try d2-d3, with the idea of pushing my g-pawn further.

4.♗g2 h6 5.d3 ♘f6 6.h3 ♗d6 7.♘d2 ♘bd7 8.♘f1 b5 9.♕c2 ♘b6 10.♘e3

For the time being, Black is playing with confidence; among other things, he's not giving me the chance to play my knight to g3.

10…♗b7 11.♗d2 a5 12.♘f3 a4 13.♖g1 a3 14.b3 ♕c7 15.c4

White could also have played h3-h4, intending g4-g5.

15…bxc4 16.dxc4 ♘bd7 17.♖c1 ♕b8 18.♘d4 0-0

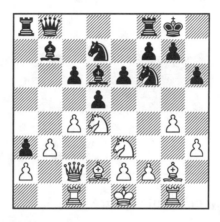

And so, Black couldn't resist: he castled. He felt uncomfortable leaving his king in the center. Why? Well, it might be because that's the way we have been taught. All the time. In all the books.

Seriously, though, what is the problem with having the king stay in the center? Clearly, it's that, when the center opens up, he might come under attack from the enemy's pieces. And also, having the king in the center prevents the rooks from coordinating. In Elshad's Opening, from the start, White doesn't plan to coordinate anything – he waits for his opponent to castle conventionally on one wing or the other, when one rook will be available on that side for a direct attack. This is unexpected, unknown strategy; and therefore, you may extract dividends from the knowledge you will gain from this book.

19.h4

A logical continuation.

Here 19.g5!? is a forceful push. Check it out yourself. In my opinion, White's attack is quite strong, e.g. 19...hxg5 20.♘g4 ♘xg4 21.hxg4 c5 22.♖h1 g6 23.♘xe6 fxe6 24.♕xg6#.

19...c5 20.♘b5 d4 21.♘f1 ♗xg2 22.♖xg2 ♘e5 23.g5 hxg5

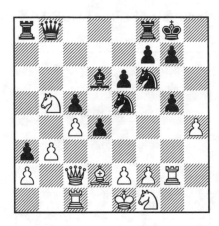

There are a few different captures on g5.

24.hxg5

Right now, I like the 24.♗xg5 recapture even more than the game move: in addition to the h-pawn battering ram, there is a direct threat. Check it out for yourself.

24...♘h5 25.♘xd6 ♕xd6 26.f4 ♘d7 27.♖h2 g6 28.♕e4

Time for the queen to start working, as well.

28...♖ab8 29.♔d1 ♖fe8 30.♔c2 e5 31.f5

Just look at that blockading square e4!

31...♘g7

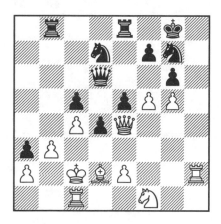

32.f6

32.♕h4! was an excellent possibility, an attacking method that deserves study: 32...♘h5 33.♘g3 ♖ed8 (33...d3+ doesn't save him; White wins with exact play, e.g. 34.exd3 e4 35.♘xe4 ♖xe4 36.dxe4 ♘e5 37.♕h3 ♖d8 38.♗a5 ♖e8 39.♖d1 ♕c6 40.♖d5) 34.fxg6 ♕xg6+ 35.♔d1 f5 36.♕xh5 ♕xh5 37.♖xh5 ♖f8 38.♔c2 f4 39.♘e4 f3 40.exf3 ♖xf3 41.♖ch1, with a decisive material and positional advantage.

32...♘xf6 33.gxf6 ♕xf6 34.♘g3 ♔f8 35.♖f1 ♕e6 36.♖h8+

36.♗g5 f5 37.♖h6 ♔f7 38.♕d5 ♕xd5 39.cxd5 c4 40.♘e4 cxb3+ 41.axb3 ♖ec8+ 42.♔d2 ♖b6 43.♖b1 a2 44.♖a1 ♖a8 45.♘c5 ♖b5 46.♘d3 ♖xd5 47.♖hh1 e4 48.♘f4 ♖b5 49.♔c2 ♖c8+ 50.♔b2 ♘e6 51.♘xe6 ♔xe6 52.♖xa2 ♔d5 53.♖a4 ♖c3 54.♖a3 ♖g3 55.♗d2 d3 56.exd3 ♖xd3 57.♖h2.

36...♔e7 37.♗g5+ ♔d7 38.♖h7 ♖g8 39.♖f6 ♕e8 40.♕c6+ ♔d8 41.♖d6#

A mate worthy of a diagram. Look at the black pieces: all of them are on the last two ranks.

6. Chashchikhin – Zakurdyayeva

immortalchess.net, 20 May 2015

1.c3 d5 2.d3 e5 3.g4

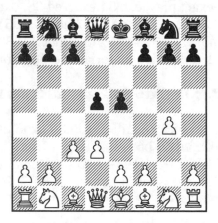

I should like to say a few more words about the players in this encounter. White was the Russian chess promoter Valery Chashchikhin. I have read some of his books, and have selected this game from his research, "The Persian Defense" (as the Elshad Opening is sometimes called). I offer him my apologies, that in my own book about the Elshad for Black, I only mentioned him in passing. Truth be told, at that moment, I did not yet have all the information.

In this game, the well known woman grandmaster Irina Zakurdyayeva played Black.

3...♗xg4

No doubt the last move was extravagant, even by Elshad standards. I'm going to suppose that White merely got confused and blundered a pawn away. But... he blundered successfully! Any similarity with Grob's Opening is purely coincidental. White's ideas here are totally different.

4.♕a4+

4.♕b3. I believe that this is stronger than the text move. White's threat against the b7-pawn forces Black to make a defensive move: 4...b6 5.♗g2 c6 6.c4 ♘f6 7.♘f3 ♗d6 8.cxd5 cxd5 9.♘c3, with compensation. It would be very difficult for Black to protect the center here. I consider White to have the upper hand. In the event of standard kingside castling, there would follow the equally standard attack down the g-file.

4...♕d7 5.♕b3 c6

That's the problem! If the queen were on d8, then ...c7-c6 would not be available to Black.

6.♘d2 ♘f6 7.♗g2 ♗d6 8.♘f1 ♘a6 9.♘g3

Absolutely the correct decision. In this position, the knight must be brought to g3. Why not to e3? Simple: the d5-pawn is overprotected by the c6-pawn. Black has a panzer pawn center; no sense in attacking armor.

9...0-0 10.♗g5 ♘e8 11.h4 ♘c5 12.♕c2 ♘e6

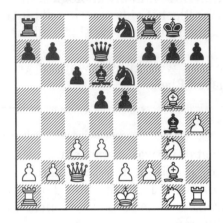

13.0-0-0

13.e4 (this possibility demonstrates White's many-faceted attacking ideas; if Black plays passively, watch what happens by the end of this variation) 13...f6 14.♗e3 dxe4 15.dxe4 ♗c5 16.♗h3 ♗xh3 17.♖d1 ♕f7 18.♘xh3 ♗xe3 19.fxe3 a5 20.0-0 a4 21.♕g2 ♖a5 22.♘g5 ♘xg5 23.hxg5 ♖b5 24.♘f5, with an attack.

13...b5 14.f3!

An excellent move! And typical for this opening. The bishop falls. Even the "machines" show an advantage for White here – hooray!

14...e4?

14...♘xg5 is instructive. Not a strictly necessary variation, it's actually not a forcing one, either: 15.hxg5 ♗e6 16.♘h5 a5 17.e4 b4 18.♗h3 bxc3 19.♕xc3 d4 20.♕d2 c5 21.♘f6+ gxf6 22.gxf6 c4 23.♕g5+ ♔h8 24.♗g4 cxd3:

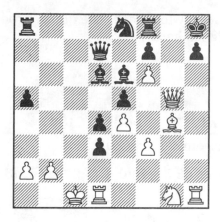

25.♘e2!! ♕c6+ 26.♘c3 dxc3 27.♖xh7+ ♔xh7 28.♖h1#.

15.fxg4

15.dxe4 is even stronger: 15...♗xg3 16.fxg4 ♘xg5 17.exd5 ♘e6 18.dxe6 ♕xe6 19.♔b1, with attack.

15...♗xg3 16.dxe4 ♘xg5 17.hxg5 ♕xg4 18.♗f3

18.exd5±.

18...♕xg5+ 19.♔b1 g6 20.exd5 cxd5 21.♖xd5 ♕e3 22.♖d3

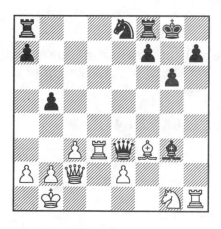

Surprise!... but only for Black. The queen's rook is definitely a goner. Black resigned here.

1-0

7. NemtsevIgor (2175) – bodlja (2104)

Live Chess Chess.com, 26 May 2015

1.c3 d5 2.♕a4+ c6 3.g4 g6 4.♗g2 ♗g7 5.d3 ♘f6 6.g5 ♘h5

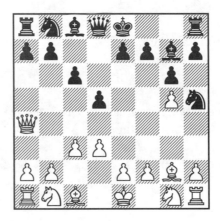

We present this game in order to showcase some important ideas.

7.♗f3

This being one of them. As a rule, no one expects this move; and so, they bravely go out to h5 with the knight to block the h-pawn's advance.

7...0-0 8.♗xh5 gxh5 9.♕h4

A classic queen transfer, after which Black can no longer save the pawn.

9...♗f5 10.♘d2

In order that soon he may remove the h5-pawn with his knight.

10...e5 11.♘f1 h6 12.♘g3

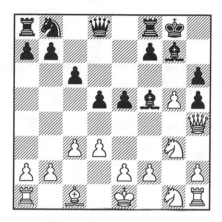

The whole point: the knight takes on h5, the g-file is opened. Unfortunately, I was unable to see my excellent plan through to victory.

12...♗g6 13.♘xh5 ♗xh5 14.♕xh5 hxg5 15.♗xg5 ♕d6 16.♘f3 ♕g6

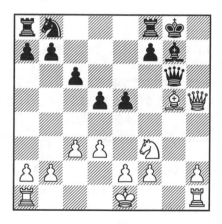

17.♕xg6

Simplest: I go for a better ending, especially with an extra pawn. Not bad, but I could have played for the attack, temporarily keeping the queens on; and this would have been stronger: 17.♕h4!?

(what I should have played) 17...f6 (17...e4 18.dxe4 dxe4 19.♘d2 ♘d7 20.0-0-0 f6 21.♗f4 ♕h7 22.♕xh7+ ♔xh7 23.♘xe4, now with two extra pawns) 18.♗e3 ♘d7 19.♖g1 ♕h7 20.♗h6 ♖f7 21.0-0-0, with a powerful attack.

17...fxg6 18.♖g1 ♘d7 19.0-0-0 ♔f7 20.♗h4 ♗f6 21.♗xf6 ♔xf6 22.♖g4 ♖g8 23.♖dg1 ♖ae8

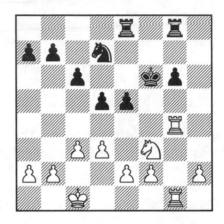

Black's pieces occupy very active positions; but alas, I was unable to win this position.

24.e4 dxe4 25.dxe4 ♘c5 26.♔c2 ♘e6 27.♖d1 ♖d8 28.♖gg1 ♘f4 29.h4 ♘h3 30.♖g3 ♘f4 31.♖g5 ♖xd1 32.♔xd1 ♖e8 33. ♔d2 ♖e6 34.♔c2 ♖e8 35.♖g4 ♖d8 36.♘e1 a5 37.♖g3 ♖h8 38.♘f3 ♘e2 39.♖g2 ♘f4 40.♖g1 ♖d8 41.♖d1 ♖xd1 42.♔xd1

There was not much time left, so I started repeating moves.

42...♘g2 43.♔e2 ♔e6 44.♘g5+ ♔d6 45.♘f3 b5 46.b3 c5 47.♔d3 ♘f4+ 48.♔e3 ♘g2+ 49.♔d3 ♘f4+ 50.♔e3 ♘g2+ 51.♔d3 ♘f4+ 52.♔e3 ½-½

8. NemtsevIgor (2166) – flowerbelly (2035)

Live Chess Chess.com, 20 May 2015

1.d3 d5 2.c3 e5 3.♘d2 f5

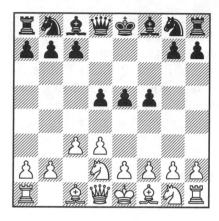

A very natural continuation, which is often seen – and why? Well, once White starts giving up the center, why shouldn't I take it?

4.h3 ♘f6 5.g4

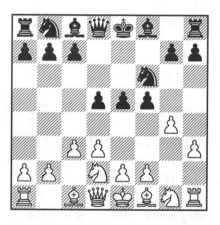

Now here's something Black definitely wasn't expecting! Not only does White move the pawn away from "where his king is headed," but he gives it up!

5…fxg4 6.hxg4!

I'm sure that I have to play it this way – even though I used to follow the Elshad "rules" with 6.♗g2.

After 6.♗g2, if Black now gets greedy with 6...gxh3, then White's play would be justified. (However, 6...g3!? 7.fxg3 now is the move for Black. It leads to a game with mutually good play; but we want the good play to be only for White.) White continues 7.♘xh3!, when it looks like Black would want to bring the bishop to e6 now; but then White's knight could jump out to g5. Now 7...h6 seems to prevent this move, but 8.♘g5! turns out to be possible – and also quite strong.

6...♗xg4 7.♗g2 c6

The panzer setup – very sensible.

8.♘f1

A magical knight maneuver. This is one of the chief paths for the horse in the Elshad Opening.

8...♗d6 9.♕a4 ♘bd7 10.♘g3

Right here. It shouldn't go to e3, since the black d5-pawn is well protected by its colleague on c6.

10...♕c7 11.f3 ♗e6 12.♘h5 ♘xh5 13.♖xh5 ♘f6 14.♖g5

It's not often that you'll see a rook like this.

14...g6 15.♗e3 b6 16.c4 d4

Black closes up the game, evidently fearing to castle short, and accordingly he castles long.

17.♗d2 0-0-0 18.b4 c5?

Looks like the fatal error.

19.bxc5 ♕xc5?! 20.f4

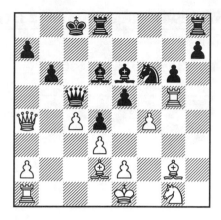

All of the doors have now been flung wide open; Black's king is clearly feeling the draft...

20...♕a3 21.♕c6+

When you're attacking the king, of course, under no circumstances should you trade queens, the queen being the most powerful weapon you have. It's like an attacking center in soccer – it ought to run and score goals.

21...♗c7 22.♕xe6+

Nyah-nyah!

22...♘d7 23.fxe5 ♖he8 24.♕c6 ♘c5 25.e6 ♕a4 26.♖xc5 bxc5 27.♕b7#

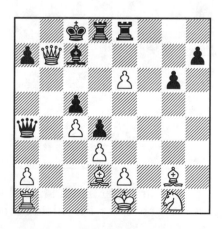

9. nemtsevguru (2294) – diaryofjane (2311)

lichess.org, 28 April 2016

1.c3 e5 2.♕a4 c6 3.g4 d5 4.h3 ♗e6

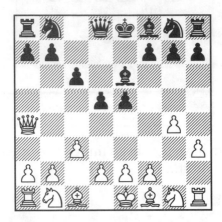

This game was played on the Lichess platform; my opponent's rating was pretty high. The move he played wasn't optimal. Why should one "support" the d5-pawn? In Elshad's Opening, this bishop frequently comes under attack by the knight from g5. So, let's remember that as soon as Black's light-squared bishop gets to e6, we send our knight to g5.

5.♗g2 ♘d7 6.d3 ♗c5 7.♘d2 ♕h4

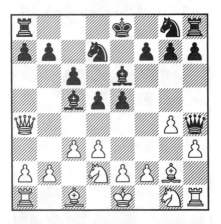

A very concrete try. On the other hand, I had already faced all of this before, so I was ready for it. Here, the "hit to the bone" is working.

8.d4! exd4 9.♘gf3

And with the knight tempo, too.

9...♕d8 10.cxd4 ♗d6 11.e4

I tell you, this is a most unusual position in this opening.

11...♘e7 12.0-0 0-0 13.e5

He doesn't want to play it well...

13...♗c7 14.♘g5

And here it is: the promised knight on g5. If Black doesn't react right away, then I will play f4-f5 too.

14...♘g6 15.♘df3

15.f4 doesn't work here: 15...♘xf4 16.♖xf4 ♕xg5.

15...c5 16.♘xe6 fxe6 17.♘g5

Threatening e6.

17...♕e7 18.♕b5 ♗b6 19.dxc5 ♗xc5 20.b4 ♗xb4 21.♘xe6

A simple little stroke, allowing me to get two powerful bishops against a pair of knights.

21...♕xe6 22.♕xb4 ♕xe5 23.♗b2 ♕g5 24.♕xb7 ♘de5 25.♕xd5

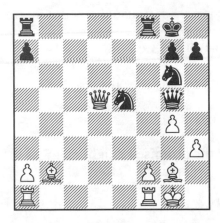

A very important moment in a blitz setting. White's position is very strong, but at this point, he has to stop and calculate the variations, even spending half a minute on it. And he will win at once.

25...♔h8 26.♖ae1 ♖ae8 27.f4

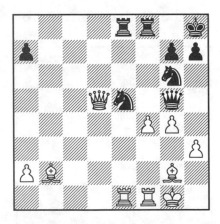

It was on this very move that a half-minute went by. The variations were not complex, but they did need to be calculated.

27...♘xf4 28.♖xe5 ♘e2+

28...♘xd5 29.♖xf8+ ♖xf8 30.♖xg5 is also hopeless for Black.

29.♖xe2 1-0

---

10. nemtsevguru (2317) – kknight (2250)

lichess.org, 31 October 2016

1.c3 c6 2.♕a4 d5 3.g4 h6

Hyper-prophylactic, against a possible g4-g5. Black prepares to bring the knight out to f6.

4.h3 ♘f6 5.♗g2 e5 6.d3 ♗d6 7.♘d2 0-0

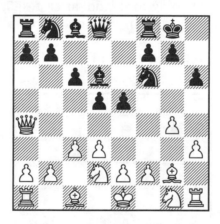

Of course, this is a daring decision. The h6-pawn is a clear target in case of an attack against the black king.

8.♘f1 ♗d7 9.♘g3

The knight heads straight for g3. First, there's no point in going to e3, what with the d5-pawn so well supported by the c6-pawn. And secondly, Black has already castled.

9...♘a6 10.g5

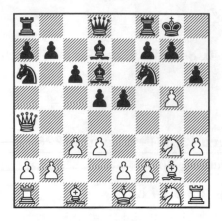

The Elshad's *tabiya* (standard starting position). I've seen this setup in the games of Elshad himself. Before this, I thought that, in this kind of position, one needed to first bring the pawn to h4, and only then play g4-g5. But there's also a different attacking formation, with the knight going to f3 and, after g4-g5, recapturing on g5. There are games like this in this book, too.

10...hxg5 11.♗xg5 ♞c5 12.♕h4

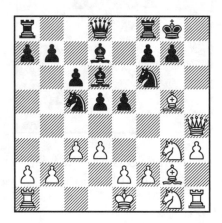

The standard – theoretical, even – queen shuttle to attack the king. Strictly speaking, this is the reason White played his queen out to a4, in order to bring it, if possible, over to the kingside.

12...♞e6 13.♗xf6

This might not be the best decision. White, of course, does obtain a positional advantage. But I could have also played the attacking move 13.♞f3!?:

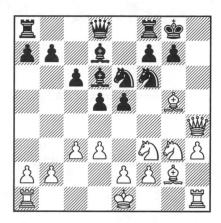

Here is what White could have tried. The idea is that after the exchange on g5, Black's knight would be tied to the f6 square to prevent checkmate on h7: 13...♞xg5 14.♞xg5 ♖e8 15.♖g1 ♛b6 16.♞h5 ♗e7 17.♞xg7 ♚xg7 18.♞e6+ ♗xe6 19.♗e4+ ♚f8 20.♛h6#.

This variation is not strictly forced, but it does show the attacking method.

13...♛xf6 14.♛xf6 gxf6 15.♞f5 ♗c7 16.e3 ♞f4?

I've managed to befuddle my opponent.

17.♞e7+ ♚g7 18.exf4 exf4 19.0-0-0 ♖fe8

Although I have to return the knight, still, White's advantage is indisputable.

20.♞xd5 cxd5 21.♗xd5 ♖ab8 22.♞f3 ♗b6 23.d4 ♗f5 24. ♖hg1+ ♚f8

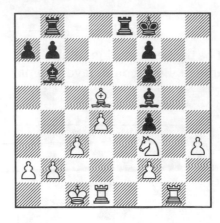

I acknowledge that, in this game, I used up a lot of time – practically as much as my opponent did – so much so, that we were already in a sort of time pressure (if such a term can be applied to a 3-minute game).

25.♘h4

White did not have to give up the file: 25.♖de1!? ♗c7 26.h4±. I'm not happy with the finish of this game. My play could have been more accurate. Anyway, the outcome was still favorable.

25...♗h7 26.♖g4? ♖e2!

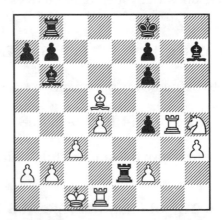

My opponent's on fire. I draw everyone's attention to this: that a real master is one who, under any circumstances, will play his rook to his seventh rank.

27.♖dg1 ♖be8 28.♗b3

28.♖g7!. This was discovered in analysis: 28...♖e1+ 29.♖xe1 ♖xe1+ 30.♔d2 ♔xg7 31.♔xe1+−. White has a 4-2 pawn majority on the queenside, which means that soon, two connected passed pawns will appear. The split pawns on the kingside can only appeal, let's say, to Bronstein.

28...♖xf2 29.♖g7

Here we had only seconds left, so I ask you not to judge us too harshly.

I might have drawn the game with 29.♗xf7, e.g. 29...♔xf7 30.♖g7+ ♔f8 31.♖xh7 ♖ee2 32.♘g6+ ♔g8 33.♖e7 f3 34.♘h4+ ♔f8 35.♘g6+ ♔g8=.

29...♖f1+ 30.♖xf1 ♔xg7 31.♖xf4 ♗c7 32.♖g4+ ♔f8 33.♘f3 ♖e3 34.♘h4 ♖xh3 35.c4 ♖h1+ 36.♔d2

When you play Internet games, sometimes you might play 10 moves within a couple of seconds. Notice that the players' ratings show that, even at such speed, they practically don't hang anything.

36...♖f1 37.c5 ♗f4+ 38.♔c3 f5 39.♖g2 ♗c7 40.♖g5 f4 41.♖h5 ♗e4 42.♘f5 ♗a5+ 43.♔c4 ♖c1+ 44.♔b5 a6+ 45. ♔xa5 f6

Here Black's time ran out. On the other hand, his position was definitely lost. **1-0**

11. nemtsevguru (2193) – zm1967 (1995)

lichess.org, 26 April 2016

1.c3 e5 2.♕a4 c6 3.g4 d5 4.h3 ♗d7

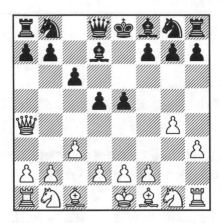

Sometimes it happens on the Internet that you play several games against the same opponent (see Game 24). Already, he is very angry: he has been defeated with White as well as Black, by the same opening. And it's all the more interesting to see how this player tries to get familiar with these positions, with an irrepressible desire to take his revenge – to win at least one game out of ten.

5.♗g2

Black's last move was played with the clear intent to advance his c-pawn to c5.

5...c5 6.♕b3 ♗c6 7.d3

It's important that my bishop already stands on g2, so that Black cannot play ...d5-d4.

7...♘f6 8.♘d2 ♗e7 9.♘f1 0-0 10.♘g3

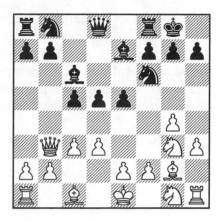

In this case, since Black has already castled, I bring the knight to g3 right away. Now I want to play g4-g5, as the black knight cannot reach the blockading square h5.

10...♘bd7 11.g5 c4 12.♕c2

We are not falling for the trap 12.dxc4? dxc4 13.♕c2 ♗xg2.

12...♘e8 13.dxc4

A forced capture: we must open the queen's diagonal to h7.

13...dxc4 14.♗xc6 bxc6 15.h4 ♗d6 16.♘f5 ♘b6 17.♘f3 ♕d7 18.♖g1 ♘d5 19.h5 ♘ec7 20.h6

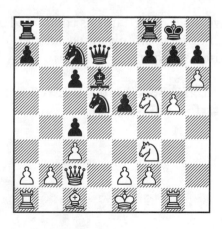

Chapter 1

What is the nature of Black's problem? He sees that his king is under direct attack. In similar situations from the Sicilian Defense, White has already castled queenside, and therefore Black can launch a counterattack against him. But here Black simply has no object for attack. The attack must, therefore, come against the center – but here there is not even a center, no collection of pawns there.

20...g6 21.♘xd6 ♕xd6 22.♘d2 ♕e6 23.♘e4 ♘e8

With the very last of his strength, Black defends the holes in the dark squares.

24.♘g3 ♕h3 25.♕e4 ♕e6 26.♕xc4 ♘d6 27.♕d3 ♘f4 28.♕f3 ♖fe8 29.♘e4 ♘xe4 30.♕xe4 ♘d5 31.♖g3 f5

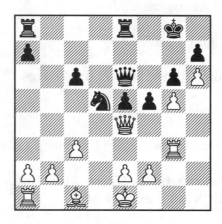

You have to give Black credit: he has conducted the defense well. But here, after ...f7-f5, we simply must take *en passant,* leaving Black's king exposed still further.

32.gxf6 *e.p.* ♘xf6 33.♕f3 e4 34.♕e3 ♘h5 35.♖g1 ♕f5 36.♕g5 ♖f8 37.♕xf5 ♖xf5 38.♗e3

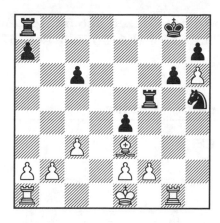

Here I suddenly realized that I had an extra pawn – and that in an ending, with pawns on both flanks, and bishop vs. knight. So why do I need to play for mate?

38...♖d8 39.♖d1 ♖xd1+ 40.♔xd1 ♖d5+ 41.♔c2 ♘f6 42.c4

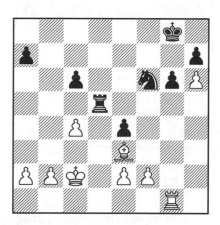

One principle of endgame play is simple: look to see where you have more pawns – in this case, an extra pawn on the queenside. That means, play on that side: create a passed pawn.

42...♖a5 43.a3 c5 44.♖d1 ♔f7 45.♖d6 ♔e7 46.♖c6 ♘d7 47.♗g5+ ♔e8 48.♖c8+ ♔f7 49.♖h8

Black defends his queenside with all his might, but now he loses material on the kingside.

49...♘f8 50.♗f4 ♖a6 51.♗e5 ♖e6 52.♗g7 ♘d7 53.♖xh7 g5 54.♗c3+ ♔g6 55.♖xd7 ♔xh6 56.♖d5 ♖c6 57.♖e5 ♔g6 58. ♖xe4 1-0

12. Natalya Ryabova – rendas

1.c3 d5 2.d3 ♗f5

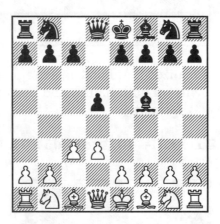

One of those errors Black often makes in the Elshad. On the other hand, this is a general error in chess. Way back when, it was Lasker who recommended bringing out your knights before your bishops. When the bishop goes out to f5, it abandons its own queenside, and – worse – becomes a target for e2-e4.

3.♕a4+ c6 4.g4 ♗d7 5.h3 c5 6.♕b3 ♗c6

And here the bishop occupies the queen's knight's spot. You cannot describe such a placement of the queenside pieces as optimal.

7.♗g2 e6 8.♘d2 ♗e7 9.♘f1

9.g5 f6 10.h4 ♕d7.

9...♗h4 10.♘f3

How sick is that?!

10…♗e7 11.g5!

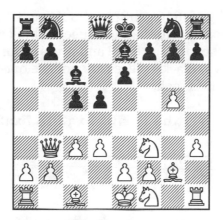

Now, *that's* strong! All by itself, the g-pawn freezes the development of Black's entire kingside.

11…f6

Opens up the light squares around the black king.

12.h4 ♕d7 13.♘g3 ♗a4

I don't think that White had noticed this threat; all the more interesting to watch, then, how honorably she gets out of the situation!

14.gxf6

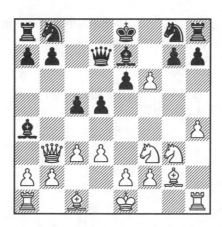

14...gxf6

14...♗xb3 15.fxg7 ♗f6 16.gxh8♕ ♗xh8 17.axb3. I think White has complete compensation for her lost queen. Think about it: she has the a-file; her bishop may go to h3 and press against e6 along with her knight from g5; Black's pieces are undeveloped; and the g-file is opened for White's rook.

15.♕a3 c4 16.b4 cxb3 17.♕b2 bxa2 18.♖xa2 ♗c6 19.♗h3

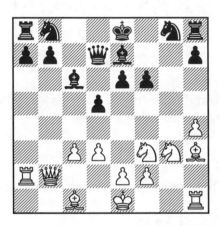

Excellent! For the pawn, White has a clear advantage: she has pressure on all the diagonals and files.

19...♕d6 20.♘d4 ♗d7 21.♕xb7 ♗c6 22.♘xc6 ♕xc6 23.♕xc6+ ♘xc6 24.♗xe6

It often happens that a positional advantage is converted into a material one. At some point, your opponent is simply unable to defend things any longer.

24...♖d8 25.♗e3 d4 26.cxd4 ♗b4+ 27.♔f1 ♘xd4 28.♗xd4 ♖xd4 29.♖xa7 ♖d8 30.♘f5

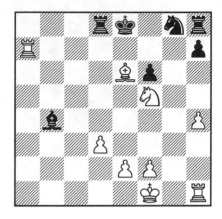

White already has two extra pawns, while Black's pieces are still in the process of development.

30..♘e7 31.♘xe7 ♗xe7 32.♖g1 ♔f8 33.h5 h6 34.♖g6 ♖b8 35.♖a4 ♖b1+ 36.♔g2 ♖b8 37.♖ag4 ♔e8 38.♖g8+ ♖xg8

38...♗f8.

39.♖xg8+ ♗f8 40.♖g6 ♖b5 41.♖xf6 ♖xh5

The game ended here; Black forfeited, apparently. But White's position is totally winning. Three connected passed pawns will rapidly be promoted. **1-0**

13. Nemtsev_Igor (2759) – Zaina_Kusya (2470)

3 May 2015

1.d3 d5 2.c3 e6 3.♘d2 c6

Perhaps my opponent intends to play the Meran System, and through force of habit sets up her pawns that way.

4.g4

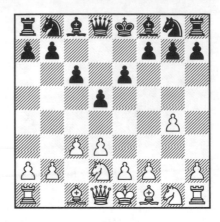

We could play cleverly with h2-h3, of course, but I wanted to try an immediate g2-g4.

4...e5 5.h3 h5

On the whole, this wasn't a bad idea; still, Black has lost a whole tempo on the e-pawn's advance.

6.gxh5 ♖xh5

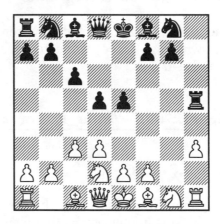

The only problem is that, when they play ...h7-h5, most players are unaware of its consequences, simply because this kind of strategic problem rarely arises. On the one hand, White gets a weak pawn at h3; on the other hand, Black can no longer castle short. Also, White does have a few ideas in this position, while Black finds herself in *terra incognita*.

7.♗g2 ♘f6 8.♘f1 ♗e6 9.♘g3

A standard maneuver in the Elshad – one, of course, unknown to the player of the black pieces. She has to retreat... but to where?

9...♖h7

From a purely psychological standpoint, Black does not wish to go back to h8 – but that was the right move here.

10.♘f3

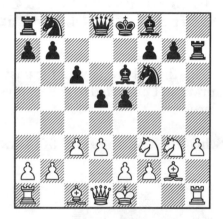

The general rule for opening structures is that, when Black's light-squared bishop goes to e6, we immediately play ♘f3, so as to then jump out to g5, hitting the bishop.

10...♗d6 11.♘g5 ♖h8 12.♘xe6 fxe6 13.a4 ♘bd7 14.a5 ♕c7 15.a6 b6

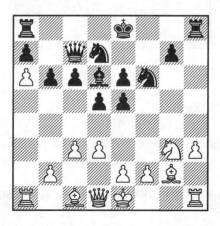

Ramming with the a-pawn is a standard technique in this open-ing; but in this case I am not satisfied with my decisions regarding e2-e4. It would be better to play h3-h4 and bring the bishop out to h3, with strong pressure on e6. I've known this well, but I wanted to try something new.

16.e4

16.h4! 0-0-0 17.♗g5 ♔b8 18.♗h3±.

16...♘c5 17.b4 ♘cd7 18.♕a4 b5 19.♕a5 ♘b6 20.♗e3 ♖b8 21.♗xb6 ♖xb6 22.♔f1 ♘d7 23.h4 ♘b8 24.♕a2 ♖xa6 25.♕b1 ♖xa1 26.♕xa1 ♔d7

I must acknowledge that all my play for the past 10 moves didn't make me at all happy. But I managed to collect myself and play the rest of the game decently.

27.h5 ♖f8 28.h6 ♕b6 29.♕e1 gxh6 30.♖xh6 ♖f7 31.♗h3

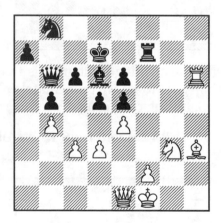

Finally!

31...♖e7 32.♕e2 c5

Black has lost sight of the board. I have a plan and Black doesn't. She rushes her moves, and miscalculates.

33.exd5 cxb4 34.♗xe6+ ♔c7 35.cxb4 ♗xb4 36.♘e4

Elshad's famous knight has re-emerged!

36...♕a5 37.♕c2+ ♔b6

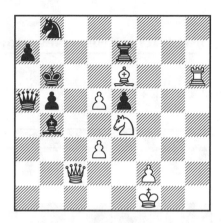

The usual rule for positions like this runs as follows: whoever first starts checking, or creating threats against the enemy king, wins. This position is no exception.

38.♗c8+

38.d6 ♕a1+ 39.♔g2 ♖g7+ 40.♘g3 ♘c6 41.d7 ♗e7 42.♗d5 ♗c5 43.♖xc6+ ♔a5 44.♕xc5 ♖xg3+ 45.fxg3 ♕b2+ 46.♕c2 ♕d4 47.♕c3+ ♕xc3 48.♖xc3 ♔b4 49.♖b3+ ♔c5 50.d8♕ a5 51.♕c7+ ♔d4 52.♖xb5 a4 53.♕c5+.

38...♖e6 39.♖xe6+ ♗d6 40.♕c5#

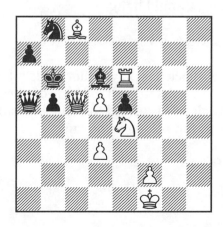

An unusual mate. I played it without even realizing that it was checkmate. That happens sometimes. When just seconds remain on the clock, sometimes you just give checks.

14. Nemtsev_Igor (2891) – Krasavtsev_Boris (2845)

19 July 2015

1.c3 d5 2.♕a4+ c6 3.g4 e5

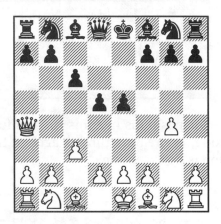

Black adopts the panzer system.

4.h3

In some sense, this is forced: Black was threatening ...b7-b5, when the pawn on g4 would hang.

4...♗d6 5.♗g2 h6 6.d3 ♘f6 7.♘d2 ♗e6

Up to this point, Black has played more or less logically; but this bishop move in no way fits in with the logic of the position. On the other hand, Black clearly is afraid to castle kingside, so he makes "developing" moves for as long as he can.

8.♘f1 ♘bd7 9.♘f3

As soon as the bishop lands on e6, it makes sense to bring out the knight to f3. Why? Everything hinges on the g4-g5 break. If it is carried out, then we can recapture with our knight, attacking the bishop with the threat of taking it off and spoiling Black's pawn structure. This could prove especially important if Black actually castles short.

9…♕c7

9…0-0?! 10.g5 hxg5 11.♘xg5, and White, along with the aforementioned capture on e6, would have the maneuver ♕a4-h4, with mating threats. Moreover, this would open the g-file for White's rook.

10.♘e3 e4

Completely logical. Black tries to strike in the center.

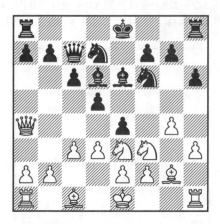

11.dxe4

Generally speaking, I immediately grab any pawn that appears on my fourth rank. There was another interesting possibility: 11.♘d4!? 0-0 12.♘ef5 ♘c5 13.♕c2 ♗xf5 14.♘xf5 exd3 15.exd3 ♖ae8+ 16.♗e3 ♘e6 17.0-0-0, when White's attack looks stronger to me.

11...♘xe4 12.♘d4 ♘dc5 13.♕c2 ♗d7 14.b4 ♘c6

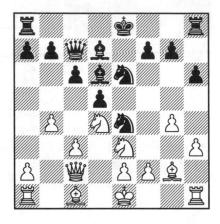

15.♘df5

A very natural decision. The position also contains the tactical trick 15.♘b5!?, for example 15...cxb5 16.♘xd5 ♕c4 17.♕xe4 ♕xe4 18.♗xe4 ♗c6 19.♗e3, with a healthy extra pawn for White – although it's true that the play here does not fit in with this opening's main ideas.

15...♗f8 16.♗xe4 dxe4 17.♕xe4 g6 18.♘d4 ♗g7 19.♗d2 0-0 20.h4 ♖ae8 21.♕d3 ♘f4 22.♕c4 b5 23.♕b3

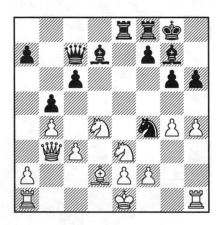

The climax of the battle. I could have taken the pawn on b5 – but, to be honest, I didn't see it (23.♘xb5! ♕e5 24.♘d4).

23...c5 24.bxc5 ♕xc5 25.h5 ♗xd4 26.cxd4 ♕xd4 27.♖c1 ♗xg4 28.hxg6 ♗xe2 29.gxf7+ ♖xf7 30.♖g1+

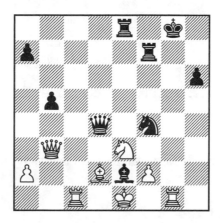

The rook enters the fray to deadly effect. Another proof of concept of this opening, in the sense that White's king, which stayed in the center, managed to survive, while Black's castled king did not.

30...♔f8 31.♗b4+ ♖ee7 32.♖c8+ 1-0

15. Nemtsev_Igor (2889) – Lukin_Sergey (2622)

16 August 2015

1.c3 d5 2.♕a4+ c6 3.g4 e5 4.h3 ♗d6 5.♗g2 h5

A fairly popular answer. If you're going to blow up the g4-pawn, better to do it with your rook still on h8.

(see diagram next page)

6.gxh5

Now this is forced. Nevertheless, as they say, it's all been seen before.

6...♖xh5 7.d3 ♗e6

And here is the "conventional" move. Moving this bishop out to e6 wasn't motivated by any particular need.

8.♘d2 ♘d7 9.♘f1

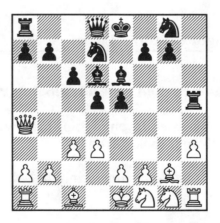

Nobody expects this move – not when they face the Elshad for the first time, anyway. The logic of this maneuver is very simple:

the knight goes to g3 to drive off the rook, to prepare the h3-h4-h5 pawn advance, and to control e4.

9...♛b6 10.♕c2

In order to enable the c1-bishop to develop to e3.

10...♞e7 11.♗e3 d4

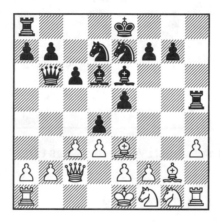

Here it is! When we have White, we especially provoke Black into playing this advance. If this were checkers, then everything would be great for Black.

12.♗d2!

This is how things look now: the pawn has gone from d5 to d4, opening up the diagonal for the g2-bishop. The knight can go through g3 to reach e4. If Black takes ...d4xc3 later on, then we recapture with b2xc3, opening the b-file for an attack. And if Black should play ...c6-c5, then we could reply c3-c4, securing the long light-squared diagonal for our fianchettoed bishop on g2. In the meantime, we keep any black pieces off d5 (12.cxd4?! exd4 13.♗d2 would open the e-file in Black's favor).

12...0-0-0 13.♞g3 ♜h7 14.♞e4 ♗c7 15.♞f3 f6

A modest move, as he cannot play 15...f5? 16.♞eg5±.

16.h4 ♚b8 17.a4

The shot is fired!

17...c5 18.a5 ♕c6 19.a6 b5

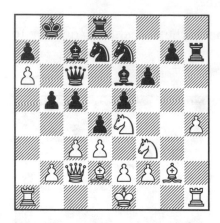

This is, of course, a bust: White now has targets to aim for – the black pawns.

20.cxd4 exd4 21.♖c1 ♗d5 22.♘xc5

Simply and tastefully done. 22.b4 cxb4 23.♕b1 ♕xa6 24.♘xd4 ♗b7 25.♕xb4 ♘d5 26.♕xb5 ♕xb5 27.♘xb5 ♘f4 28.♘xc7 ♘xg2+ 29.♔f1 ♘xh4 30.♘e6 ♖e8 31.♘f4 f5 32.♘g3 ♗xh1 33.♘xh1.

22...♕xc5 23.♕xc5 ♘xc5 24.♖xc5 ♗b6 25.♗f4+ ♔a8 26.♖xb5 ♖hh8 27.♔d2

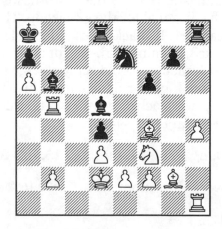

In the endgame, the king must be centralized. But in the Elshad Opening, it's always in the center!

27…♖he8 28.♖c1 ♖c8 29.♖xd5

An uncomplicated bit of tactics. It's obvious that Black's king is terribly placed on a8, and the g2-bishop has a keen interest in it.

29…♘xd5 30.♖xc8+ ♖xc8 31.♘xd4

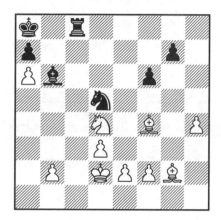

A sweet position: Black's pieces are all piled together!

31…♖d8

From this point, everything is forced.

32.♘e6 ♖d7 33.h5 ♗a5+

What else?

34.♔d1 f5 35.♘xg7 ♖xg7 36.♗xd5+ ♖b7 37.axb7#

It was on account of such finales that Elshad thought up his opening!

16. Ryabova – NN

1.c3 d5 2.d3 ♘f6 3.♕a4+ ♗d7 4.♕b3 b6

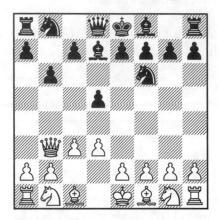

Afraid of dropping a pawn, Black weakens the long diagonal.

5.♘d2 a5 6.h3 e6 7.g4 ♗c6 8.♗g2 ♗d6 9.♘gf3 ♕d7 10.♕c2

Competently played. White waits for Black to castle.

10...0-0 11.♘f1

11.♔f1 ♘a6 12.g5 ♘e8 13.h4 f5 14.h5 e5.

11...♘a6 12.g5

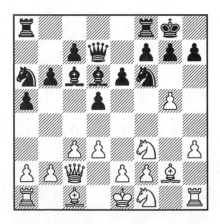

Now the direct attack begins. From one angle, it might look like White is attacking with a small force. But the fact of the matter is that, on the kingside, she does have a rook, which has already joined in the offensive from its starting square.

12...♞e8 13.h4 f5 14.h5

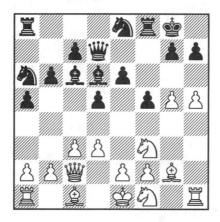

Very thematic, soon leading to a nice checkmate. There was also an alternative: 14.gxf6 ♞xf6 15.♗h3 ♞c5 16.♖g1 ♕e7 17.♗h6. You can see how freely White's attack develops.

14...e5 15.♞e3 e4 16.dxe4 dxe4??

Of course it's strange that Black didn't want to open up the f-file for his rook – and that he now allows a mating attack typical of the Elshad.

17.♕b3+

For many, this check turns out to be unexpected.

17...♚h8 18.♞h4 ♗f4

Black simply fails to see the straightforward threat. On the other hand, there doesn't seem to be a decent defense anymore.

19.♘g6+ hxg6 20.hxg6+ ♗h2 21.♖xh2#

17. Elshad – Werner

1.c3 d5 2.d3

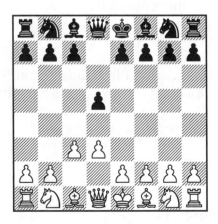

This way of playing the Elshad is different in principle, as there is no queen check from a4.

2...e5 3.g3

This move is highly uncharacteristic of the opening – an experiment. On the other hand, within a few moves, the position becomes quite "theoretical."

3...♗e6 4.h3

Playing this way leads many players into error.

4...g6 5.♘d2 f5

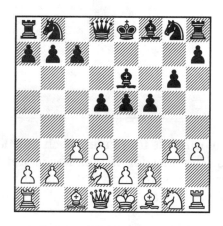

6.g4!

Aha – what's this? Black is in utter confusion. Why not take the pawn, he thinks...

6...fxg4 7.hxg4 ♗xg4 8.♗g2 c6 9.♘f1

A standard maneuver: the knight is headed for e3 or g3. In the present case, since the d5-pawn is defended by the c-pawn, there's no sense in going to e3.

9...♗g7 10.♕b3 ♕b6 11.♕a4 ♗f5

This bishop is frequently overlooked in blitz play.

12.♘g3 ♗d7

Too many bishop moves, wouldn't you say? Who violates the principles of development in the opening like this?

13.♘f3 ♘a6 14.♗e3 ♛xb2

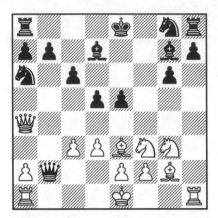

I have my own principle for playing such positions, worked out over many years. The question is whether or not to take that b2-pawn. My prescription is as follows: if, after the reply ♖b1, White can take your b7-pawn back, then you can't take his on b2.

15.0-0 ♛xc3 16.♖ab1 ♘c5 17.♛h4 ♛a5 18.d4 ♘e6

This is forced: 18...exd4? 19.♗xd4 ♗xd4 20.♛xd4 0-0-0 21.♛xh8.

19.♖xb7

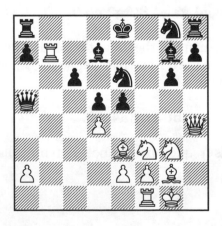

The b7-pawn has fallen, and it is evident to the naked eye that Black's king is already mouthing prayers, without understanding how he got himself into this predicament.

19...♗c8 20.♖xg7 ♘xg7 21.dxe5 ♕c7 22.♗c5 ♘e7 23.♕f6 ♘ef5 24.♘g5 ♘xg3 25.fxg3 ♗f5 26.e3 h6 27.♖xf5 gxf5 28.♕g6+ ♔d8 29.♘f7+ ♔c8 30.♕xg7 ♔b7 31.♘d6+

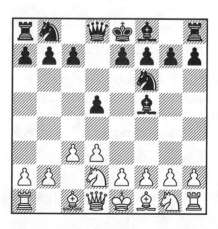

1-0

18. Nemtsev_Igor (2170) – bodlja (2109)

Live Chess Chess.com, 26 May 2015

1.d3 d5 2.c3 ♘f6 3.♘d2 ♗f5

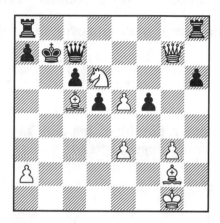

I played several games with this opponent on that day. For this game, he decided to play something different from before; however, this setup favors White, as on f5 the bishop comes under pawn attack after h2-h3 and g3-g4, the main feature of this opening. He simply was unaware of this theme in the Elshad.

4.h3 e6 5.g4 ♗g6 6.♗g2 ♗e7 7.♘f1 ♘bd7 8.♘f3 c6 9.♘g3 ♗d6 10.g5 ♘h5 11.♘xh5 ♗xh5 12.♗e3 ♕c7 13.a4

White has more useful waiting moves, in order to force Black into castling.

13...0-0 14.a5

Sometimes you just want to "eat up" a pawn on a7 if the rook leaves a8 for the center. But the main point is to clear the way for my rook to head for the kingside via a4.

14...e5 15.♘h4 d4

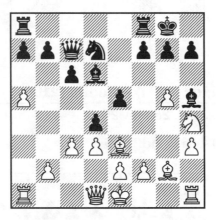

A typical attack on the bishop. We don't ever take on d4 here because it would open the e-file for Black. It's always better to retreat the bishop to d2, because now we have e2-e4, and also because sometimes the white queen can join in the attack via the b3 square.

16.♗d2 g6 17.♗e4 ♘c5 18.f3!?

An original idea. I won't miss the bishop; the main idea is to wall in Black's dark-squared bishop.

18...♘xe4 19.fxe4 c5 20.♕b3 b6 21.♘f3 ♖ab8 22.c4 bxa5 23.♕c2 ♖b7 24.♗xa5 ♕d7 25.♗d2 ♖fb8 26.♖a2 ♖b3 27.♗c1 ♗e7 28.♖h2 f6

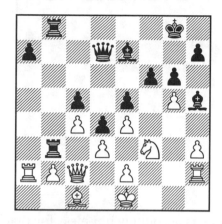

Perhaps Black should simply have stood in place. Here, we always take on f6.

29.gxf6 ♗xf6 30.♖a6 ♖3b6 31.♕a4 ♖xa6 32.♕xa6 ♖f8 33.♗h6 ♗g7 34.♗xg7 ♔xg7 35.♘xe5

Thank you!

35...♕c7 36.♕e6 ♖f6 37.♕d7+

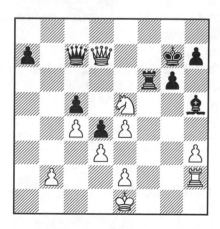

A flawless transition into an endgame. Black still has some weak pawns and the hunt for them begins.

37...♕xd7 38.♘xd7 ♖c6 39.♖f2 ♖c7 40.♘f6 ♖b7 41.♘xh5+ gxh5 42.♖f5

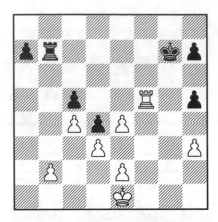

The rook ending is absolutely hopeless for Black: there are way too many weaknesses. If I can net the pawns on c5 and d4, the avalanche will wipe out everything in its path.

42...♖xb2 43.♖xc5 ♖a2 44.♖xh5 a5 45.♖d5 a4 46.♖xd4

Right on time!

46...a3 47.♖d7+ ♔f6 48.♖a7

Now that I have succeeded in getting my rook behind Black's passed pawn, it's all over.

48...h5 49.♔f2 ♖c2 50.♔e3 a2 51.h4 ♔e6 52.♖a5 ♔d6 53.e5+ ♔c6 54.♔d4 ♔b6 55.♖a3 1-0

19. nemtsevguru (2382) – centroman (1704)

lichess.org, 6 May 2017

1.c3 c6 2.♕a4 d5 3.d3 ♗f5

Nothing to be done. Habit has definitely taken up residence in the heads of chessplayers. They all play the Slav Defense, without regard for the specifics of the position.

4.h3 e6 5.g4 ♗g6 6.♗g2 ♗d6 7.♘d2 ♘d7 8.♘f1 ♘gf6 9.♘e3 0-0 10.h4

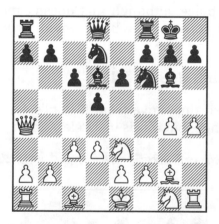

Up until this move, it might appear that everything is in order for Black: all the pieces are developed and his king is securely sheltered. But what is he going to do now? White threatens to play h4-h5, snaring Black's bishop.

10...h6

If 10...h5, then 11.gxh5 opens the g-file.

11.g5 ♘e8 12.h5 ♗h7 13.gxh6 gxh6 14.♘g4

This is where having the knight on e3 comes in handy. Black has nothing to defend the h-pawn with, and the black king, protected so well just a little while ago, isn't so safe anymore, is he?

14...♘ef6 15.♘xh6+ ♔h8 16.♗g5 ♕b8 17.♕h4

A standard choice, although that doesn't make it any more "normal" for Black. As a rule, Black would be encountering this situation for the first time.

17...♗e7 18.♘f3 ♕d8 19.♔d2

I appropriated this move from Elshad's games. One can, of course, castle long – but this is more elegant.

19...♘g8 20.♘xg8 ♗xg5+ 21.♘xg5 ♔xg8 22.♖ag1

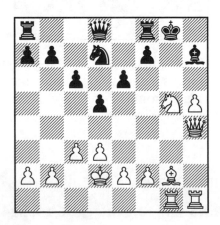

It often happens that, right about this time, our opponent falls into a sort of hypnotic trance. He is so sure that our king is weak, being stuck in the center. But look carefully: whose king is actually under assault?

22...♔h8 23.♗f3 f6 24.♘xe6

Black simply "wakes up." It's how most of these games typically end: the pressure that this opening exerts on our opponents produces this kind of result. They just start giving everything away – among other things, when their time starts to run low.

24...♕e7 25.♘xf8 ♕xf8 26.h6 ♘e5 27.♖g7 ♘xf3+ 28.exf3 ♖e8 29.♖hg1 ♖e7 30.♕f4 ♕e8 31.♕xf6 ♖e2+ 32.♔d1

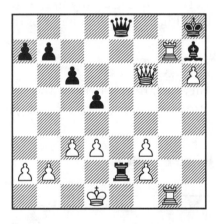

The checks have run out, and there's no more defense against ♖g8. **1-0**

20. Natalya Ryabova – Uitwisser (1570)

6 June 2017

1.c3 d5 2.d3 e5 3.♘d2 ♘f6 4.h3 ♗d6 5.g4

Natalya Ryabova is a player of amateur rank; we met on the Vkontakte social-media site. She sends me her games there. Among those, you will find some that are fully in the spirit of the Elshad, and they are not bad. I have included a few of them in this book.

5...0-0 6.♗g2

Natalya plays this variation mostly without her queen's going to a4. Now White threatens g4-g5, and the d5-pawn starts feeling uncomfortable.

6...♗e6 7.♘f1 ♘c6 8.♘e3

Very competent! Again, that threat of g4-g5.

8...♗c5 9.b4 ♗b6

9...♗d6.

10.b5 ♘e7 11.♘f3

Hitting the e5-pawn.

11...♕d6 12.a4

Outstanding! And if it wants to, even the bishop can join in from a3. And, of course, there's a4-a5.

12...♗a5 13.♗d2 h6 14.g5

Right again! Once again, the h6-pawn is the hook that White's kingside attack hangs on.

14...♘h5 15.gxh6 gxh6 16.♖g1

And so the g-file comes open, with the king's rook taking up an attacking position.

16...♘f4 17.♘g4

Maybe here she could have dropped her bishop back to h1?

17...♗xg4 18.hxg4 ♘xg2+ 19.♖xg2 e4 20.♘d4

99

In positions like this, I always recommend taking the e-pawn first. Why? Because then the e-file stays closed, and Black can't open it for his rooks (20.dxe4 dxe4 21.♘d4).

20...♕e5?!

Here is where Black should have played 20...exd3 21.exd3 ♖ae8, with a double-edged game.

21.♔f1 ♕f6 22.g5

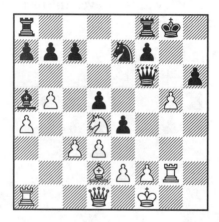

Now it's all over for Black: he walked right into the battering ram.

22...♕e5 23.gxh6+ ♔h7 24.♖g7+ ♔h8 25.♔g2 ♖g8 26.♕h1 ♘g6 27.♖g1 e3 28.♗xe3 ♗xc3 29.♘f3 ♘f4+ 30.♔f1 d4 31. ♘xe5

Yes, Black hung his queen. But he was actually forced into it! He had long since lost sight of the board, in a flood of light, and no longer understood anything that was going on.

1-0

21. Nemtsev – Kretov

Chess.com

1.c3 d5 2.♕a4+ c6 3.d3 e5 4.h3 ♗d6 5.g4 ♘e7

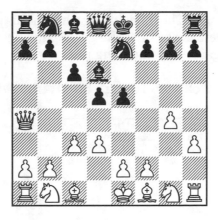

This game was played in a rapid tournament at Sokolniki Park in Moscow. Shamefully, I cannot remember my opponent's name. In that regard, it turns out that there are several good players in Moscow with the same last name.

6.♗g2 ♘d7

I should point out that my opponent was playing quite correctly. He developed his knight to e7, which is correct, since later on this knight could come out via g6 to f4 or h4. Moreover, Black is right not to castle, otherwise the game might proceed something like 6...0-0 7.♘d2 ♘d7 8.♕c2 a5 (8...♘g6) 9.♘f1 ♖e8 10.♘g3 ♘f8 11.♘f3 ♗e6 12.♘g5.

7.♘d2 h6

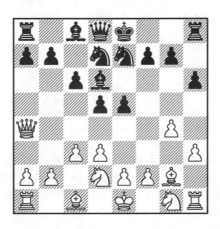

But this is a target. The reflexive advance of this pawn to h6 looks to Black like a defense against the g4-g5 advance; still, he had to find a defense against my battering ram.

8.♘f1 ♘c5 9.♕c2 ♘e6 10.♘g3 a5 11.♘h5 ♔f8

You wouldn't call such a decision normal. Apparently, Black thought that his h8-rook would be an additional defender against g4-g5.

12.♘f3 ♘c5 13.♖g1

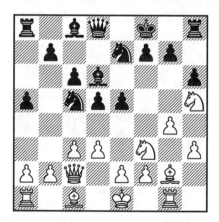

I think that Nimzowitsch would have been pleased here. At first sight, this is a "mysterious" move by the rook. But the thing is that Black has already opened the window, showing where his king is, and now we have only to come at him.

13...♘d7 14.e4 g6 15.♘g3 ♔g7 16.♘h4 d4 17.♗h1 ♘f6 18.cxd4 exd4 19.f4 ♗b4+ 20.♔f1 ♘d7 21.♕e2 ♔h7

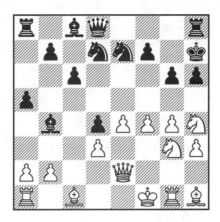

There's no place to run now. An avalanche by White's pawns and pieces like this merely has to find an opening for a decisive breakthrough.

22.e5 ♘f8 23.f5 ♖g8 24.♗e4 ♘d5 25.♘f3

Let's not hang our knight.

25...♗e7 26.h4 ♗xh4

Despair. Clearly it's dangerous to open the h-file. Perhaps it dawned on Black that there simply was nothing better.

27.♘xh4 ♕xh4 28.♖h1! ♕xg3

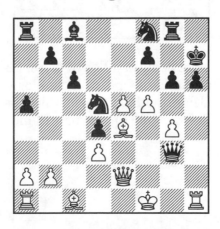

A few minutes passed while I calculated the variations.

29.♗xh6 ♖g7

The threat was 30.♗xf8, with mate.

30.♗f4+ ♔g8 31.♗xg3

White is a queen up.

31...♘e3+ 32.♔f2 c5 33.e6 fxe6 34.f6 ♖f7 35.♗e5 ♗d7 36.♕f3 ♗c6 37.♕h3 ♗xe4 38.♕h8#

22. Shmatkov – Sergeev

1998

1.c3 d5 2.♕a4+ ♘d7

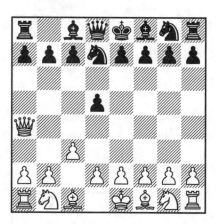

The white pieces are being handled by one of Elshad's friends, an advocate of the line. Black's ...♘b8-d7 looks illogical, but elsewhere in this book you will find another game in which Elshad plays White, which proceeded like this one for the first 18 moves.

3.g4 ♘f6 4.g5

Of course!

4…♘e4 5.d3 ♘d6

Clearly Black sees things differently from White here. He believes that his knights stand solidly in the center, while White is shoving his pawns forward willy-nilly.

6.h4 e5 7.♘d2 ♗e7 8.b4

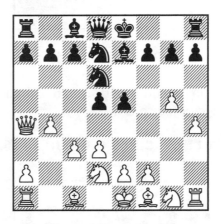

While this move echoes Elshad's play, here it is not in order, as there is no black knight on c6 and the b4-pawn won't be advancing to b5 with tempo gain. In addition, the fourth rank is now closed, preventing the white queen from redeploying to the kingside. On the other hand, Black is afraid to castle short and – paradoxical as it may seem – will shortly castle long in the face of the b-pawn's action.

8…a6 9.♕c2 ♘f8

9…♔f8.

10.♗g2

Everything is in order for White. The d5-pawn already requires defending. The simplest way would be ...c7-c6, but for some reason there are many who defend it with ...♗e6, thinking that this way they're developing another piece.

10...♗e6 11.♖b1 ♕d7 12.♗b2 0-0-0 13.a4 f6 14.b5

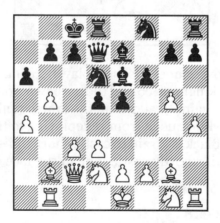

A typical line-opening device. Who cares about losing a pawn this way!

14...axb5 15.axb5 fxg5 16.♖a1 ♕xb5

When White's rook left the b-file, Black evidently thought that now would be a good time to snap off that pawn.

17.♘gf3 e4 18.c4

Well of course – in a position like this, no one could retreat! Forward, only forward! A fascinating finish is in store.

18...dxc4 19.dxc4 ♕f5 20.c5 exf3 21.c6!

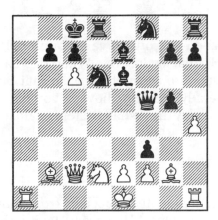

A spectacular queen sacrifice! Of course, the queen cannot be taken due to mate.

21...bxc6

21...♕xc2 22.♖a8#.

22.♕xc6 ♘d7 23.♖a7 ♘b5 24.♕b7#

23. nemtsevguru (2382) – Radu999 (1641)

lichess.org, 6 June 2017

1.c3 c6 2.♕a4

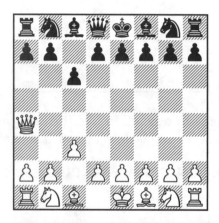

Lately, more and more often I've encountered people trying to play the Elshad System against me. When this happens, you need to get your queen out to a4 right away, so that Black can't do the same thing. Generally speaking, how do you handle it when your opponent wants to play the Elshad System against you? Now that's a question.

2...d5 3.d3 ♗f5

A reaction I see frequently, especially from those who are used to playing the Slav Defense. However, playing the bishop out to f5 has more drawbacks than benefits, for White is readying his "prime" pawn advances h2-h3 and g2-g4, when the black bishop will be harassed with tempo gain.

4.h3 e6 5.g4 ♗g6 6.♗g2 ♘d7 7.♘d2 ♗d6 8.♘f1 h6

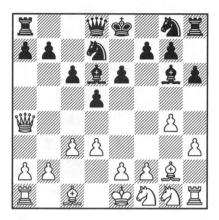

Black plays it close to the vest. But I don't have much respect for his last move. Apparently, he wants to make room for his bishop's retreat, according to the "book." But in the Elshad Opening, a pawn on h6 usually becomes a target for an attack on Black's castled position.

9.♘e3 ♘gf6 10.♘f3 0-0 11.g5

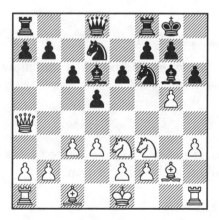

There's no reason to wait – we want that pawn on h6 right away. Another important thing is that White's rook has the g-file. Black's reply is pretty much forced, as otherwise White will take on h6.

11...hxg5 12.♘xg5 b5

Yet another typical reaction by Black. He thinks that White's queen will have to retreat to either c2 or b3.

13.♕h4

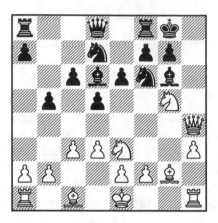

But it goes to h4! This carries out one of the major ideas of this variation, transferring the queen to the kingside via the maneuver ♕d1-a4-h4.

13...♘h5

An attempt to blockade, and perhaps somehow to pin the white knight against the queen.

14.♘g4

Building up for the assault. Once White brings the rook to g1, a breakthrough will undoubtedly turn up.

14...♖e8 15.♗f3 ♔f8

"Where are you going?" ask the white pieces of the black king, with feigned politeness...

16.♘h7+

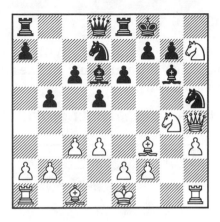

The rest requires no commentary.

16...♗xh7 17.♕xh5 ♗g6 18.♕h8+ ♔e7 19.♕xg7 ♖g8 20. ♗g5+ ♘f6 21.♗xf6+ ♔d7 22.♕h6 ♕e8 23.♗d4 c5 24.♘f6+ ♔c7 25.♘xe8+ 1-0

24. nemtsevguru (2207) – zm1967 (1985)

lichess.org, 26 April 2016

1.c3 d5 2.♕a4+ ♕d7

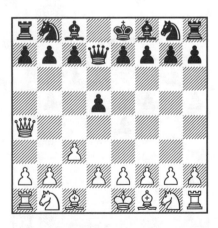

To say the least, this is no routine solution. I decided to sidestep to f4; retreating to b3 or c2 would not have been so good – Black's queen does not stand well at d7 anyway, and will have to move somewhere else eventually.

3.♕f4 c6 4.h3 ♕d6 5.♕xd6

Now is not the time to be stubborn. With the queens gone, we might reach a completely normal game; and besides, Black will be saddled with doubled pawns.

5...exd6 6.g4 ♗e6 7.♗g2 g6 8.d3 ♗g7 9.♘d2 ♘e7 10.a4

Since it's harder to conduct a mating attack with the queens off, I'll try to disrupt Black's position by attacking with my wing pawn.

10...♘d7 11.a5 a6 12.♘f1 ♘e5 13.♘f3 ♘xf3+ 14.♗xf3 ♖c8 15.♘g3 h6 16.e4

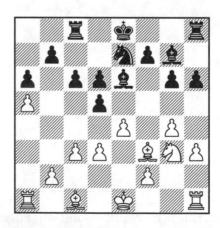

Very logical. The c3-pawn forms an impassable barrier for the fianchettoed black bishop, and that's what matters here. We are attacking his center.

16...dxe4 17.♘xe4 d5

That's it, then: Black has held on for as long as he could. Of course, there was a defense: he didn't have to hang anything. Nonetheless (and I want to stress this), when your opponent faces an opening like this for the first time, the tension and the confusion keep mounting, until at some point he loses his way through the maze.

18.♘d6+ ♚d7 19.♘xc8 ♜xc8 20.♗e3 c5 21.0-0

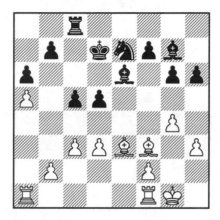

It's truly a rare occasion when Elshad castles in his games. I do it more often. Time to make use of the extra exchange.

21...♘c6 22.♜fe1 ♘e5 23.♗g2 ♜c7 24.d4 ♘c4 25.dxc5 ♘xe3 26.♜xe3 ♜xc5 27.♜d3 ♜b5 28.b4 ♚e7 29.♜ad1

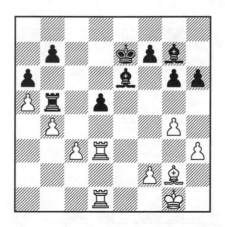

This is what I was saying before. As endgame theory counsels, I've hit him several times and created a weakness.

29...♗e5 30.♗xd5 ♗xd5 31.♖xd5 ♖xd5 32.♖xd5 ♗xc3 33.b5 ♗xa5 34.bxa6 1-0

25.Nemtsev_Igor (2913) – Master_Dizaster (2639)

16 August 2015

1.c3 c6 2.♕a4 d5 3.g4 b5

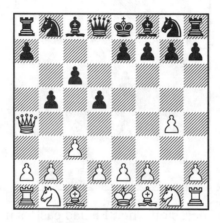

A concrete move, at any rate. Of course, Black drives the queen away from a4 – but to what end? White was planning to do that anyway – Black just didn't know that.

4.♕f4 h6 5.a4

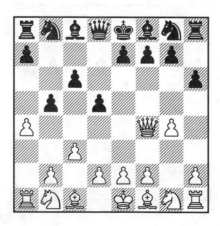

A standard blow against the sort of pawn structure Black has adopted. Generally speaking, Black's play comes off as impulsive.

5...♘f6 6.axb5 ♗xg4 7.bxc6 ♘xc6 8.d3 e5 9.♕g3 ♗d6 10.h3 e4

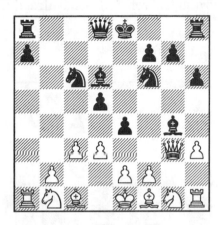

Since the queenside is totally opened up, the possibility that Black will castle short has increased dramatically. The break that Black has instituted is correct, and very good.

11.♗f4 ♗xf4 12.♕xf4 ♗e6 13.dxe4 dxe4 14.♘d2 0-0 15.♗g2 ♘e7 16.♘xe4 ♘xe4 17.♗xe4

White has an extra pawn, but to call this a won position would be premature. It needs to be stabilized and, if possible, I have to trade queens.

17...♖b8 18.♘f3 ♘g6 19.♕d2 ♕f6 20.♘d4 ♖fd8 21.♖xa7

White has won a second pawn, but the position is still full of fight.

21...♘f4 22.e3 ♘d5 23.♗xd5 ♗xd5 24.♖g1 ♗f3 25.♕c2 ♗h5 26.♕f5

Here I breathed a sigh of relief, as I had already seen the coming combination.

26...♕h4 27.♖g4

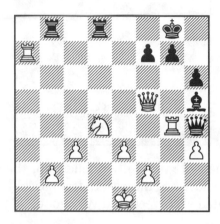

27...♗xg4 28.♕xf7+ 1-0

26. Elshad – Abelev

June 1999

1.c3 d5 2.♕a4+ c6 3.g4 e5 4.h3 ♗d6 5.d3 ♗e6

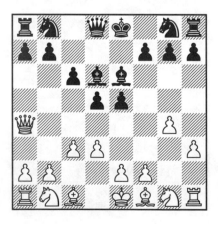

We have seen Black play this move a number of times; it probably has something to do with an internal esthetic of the person playing Black. Look here – the two bishops, standing side by side in the center. Isn't that nice?

But the reality is much different. On e6, the bishop may come under attack from a knight on g5. In the opening, we must strive to bring out the knights before the bishops. Why? Well, back in his day, the great Emanuel Lasker advised us to do it this way. What is the bishop doing on e6, concretely? It defends and supports the d5-pawn, right? But this pawn is already held by the pawn at c6?! Here is a general rule in chess: pawns should be protected by pawns; and as a matter of course, when a thing must be defended, it should be defended by the weakest possible fighting unit available. This is so that the stronger chessmen can undertake some activity instead of standing guard over pawns.

6.♗g2

It might seem strange to develop the king's bishop thus, since it is running straight into the protected pawn on d5, but the idea is to clear the f1 square for the knight.

6...♘d7 7.♘d2 ♘e7 8.♘f1 ♘g6 9.♘f3

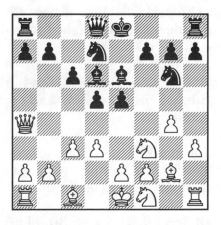

An important principle of Elshad's Opening, with the black bishop at e6, is to bring one's knight out to g5 as quickly as possible.

9...♘c5 10.♕c2 e4 11.dxe4

A forced capture in almost every similar situation. The general principle is: we remove any black pawn that appears on the fourth rank.

11...♘xe4 12.♘d4 ♘c5 13.♗d2 ♘h4 14.♘e3 ♗f4 15.♖g1 ♗h2 16.♖f1 ♗f4 17.♗h1 h5

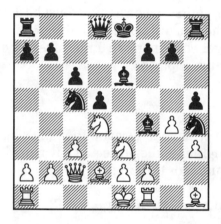

I believe that Black outsmarted himself here. Generally speaking, it's a good thing to trade off White's light-squared bishop. Apparently, he disagreed.

18.0-0-0 hxg4 19.♘xe6 ♘xe6 20.♕a4 b5 21.♕a6 ♕b6 22.♕a3 0-0-0 23.hxg4 ♘c5 24.♘c2 ♗xd2+ 25.♖xd2 ♖he8 26.♖fd1 ♘e4 27.♗xe4

This is where ignoring White's bishop tells: it has knocked off a more important piece. What's important is not which pieces you trade off, but which pieces remain on the board!

27...♖xe4 28.f3 ♖e5 29.♕b4 ♘g6 30.a4 a6 31.a5

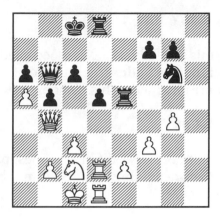

Now if the queen retreats, then White sneaks in on the dark squares. On the other hand, the move Black actually plays is worse.

31...c5 32.axb6 cxb4 33.♘xb4 ♔b7 34.♘xd5 1-0

27. Elshad – NN

1997

1.c3 d5 2.♕a4+ ♘d7 3.g4 ♘gf6 4.g5

We have seen this position before. When playing this way, Black probably doesn't seriously believe that White's pawns will be attacking so fiercely.

4...♘e4 5.d3 ♘d6 6.h4 e5

Let's examine this carefully. Black has occupied the center with pawns, which will soon be under fire. But the black knights stand very poorly: they are obstructing his bishops!

7.♘d2 ♗e7 8.b4 a6

How can different people, at different times, play all the same moves? What is Black defending against? Can it be that he's preparing to attack the queen?

9.♕c2 ♘f8 10.♗g2 ♗e6 11.♖b1 ♕d7 12.♗b2

Very clever! It appears that White does not intend to attack the queenside, so Black immediately castles there.

12...0-0-0 13.a4 f6 14.b5 axb5 15.axb5 fxg5 16.c4

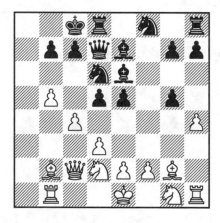

In Game 22, in this position Shmatkov played 16.♖a1. Elshad opts to open the long diagonal for his bishop.

16...g4 17.♖a1 ♕e8

Else it's mate on a8. Or if 17...♔b8, then simply 18.♕a4.

18.cxd5 ♗f5 19.♖a8+ ♔d7

Black Plays ...d7-d5, Thinking "Closed Game"

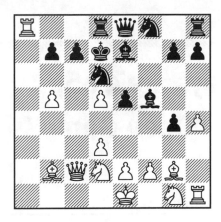

The black army, standing lethargically, is unable to save its own king. Find the pretty mate!

20.♕c6+! bxc6 21.bxc6#

Chapter 2

//

Black Plays ...e7-e5, Thinking "Open Game"

28. Elshad – A. Gorbatov

1998

1.c3 e5

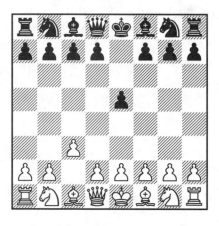

One of Black's most natural replies. As theory says, Black replies to White's strange opening move by playing in the center. However, right here we have a bit of a surprise for Black. What if Black doesn't usually play 1...e5 in reply to 1.e4 ? The point is that, in the Elshad Opening, we can do transitions and transformations of the position into more or less familiar ones – here, for example, to the Ponziani Opening. In other words, if the player of Black usually replies to 1.e4 with the Sicilian Defense, then he will soon find himself in completely unfamiliar territory...

2.♕a4

And here, one of the main ideas in the Elshad comes onstage. And what does it consist of? Not least in line: the psychological effect. White's play reminds most experienced players of a beginner's efforts. Well, let them keep on thinking that way. Why does the queen come out to a4, anyway? It's planning to head over to the kingside. Yes, indeed – along the fourth rank!

But that is not all. The queen supports a pair of important pawn advances: to e4, and to g4. Additionally, Black cannot occupy the center totally with pawns (for now, ...d7-d5 is unavailable). Not for the last time, the queen draws fire. Black wants to drive it off, to catch it...

2...♘f6

Simple and strong. Black develops according to Lasker's precepts.

3.e4

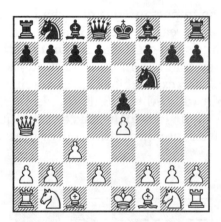

This is an important fork in the road for the theory of the Elshad. The position reached is reminiscent of the Ponziani. But Elshad has given it a different reading, lots of new ideas. Play develops according to a totally different scenario if White plays 3.g4 instead of 3.e4. That's a separate variation, whose games we will also examine in this book very carefully.

3...♘c6

All according to book. The knight is out; now, if he gets the chance, Black will seize the rest of the center by ...d7-d5.

4.♘f3 ♗c5

Oddly, Black lays this piece in the path of d2-d4. Not every piece movement from its initial square can be called development.

4...d5 (this might be considered premature) 5.♘xe5 ♘xe4 6.♘xc6 ♕d7 (the only move that doesn't lose: 6...bxc6? 7.♕xc6+ ♗d7 8.♕xd5±; or 6...♗d7?? 7.♘xd8 ♗xa4 8.♘xb7) 7.d3 ♘c5 8.♕c2 ♕xc6 9.d4 ♘e4 10.♗d3 ♗e7 (10...♗f5?? 11.f3+−) 11.♘d2 f5 12.0-0 0-0 13.♖e1±. White has a clear edge, since he will soon chase the black knight off e4 with f2-f3 and occupy the e5 square. A white knight would look much better on e5!

5.♗b5!?

This contains an important idea of Elshad's: d2-d4. The threat against the e5-pawn is real. The reply 5...a7-a6 isn't even a counterthreat, due to White's pin on the a-file. On the other hand, objectively I have to say that the immediate d2-d4 would have been stronger: 5.d4!? exd4 6.cxd4 ♗b4+ 7.♗d2! (forcing Black to take on d2) 7...♗xd2+ 8.♘bxd2 0-0 9.♗d3 d6 (9...d5 10.e5) 10.0-0±, and White's advantage is obvious to the naked eye; he just needs to prepare and carry out a center breakthrough, or press along the c-file.

5...0-0

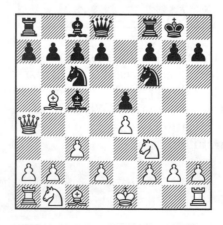

6.d4 exd4

6...♗b6 7.0-0! ♘xe4 8.dxe5 ♘c5 9.♕c2 d6 10.b4 ♘e6 11.exd6 ♕xd6 12.♖d1 ♕e7 13.♗d3 h6 14.a4 a5 15.b5 ♘b8 16.♘bd2±, with a clear advantage for White. Black has no strong points in the center for his minor pieces, while White's threats of ♗a3 or c3-c4 are serious.

7.e5 ♘g4?

A mistake. He could have tried to pin White's e-pawn along the file with his rook: 7...♖e8 8.cxd4 ♗b4+ 9.♘c3 ♘e4 10.♕b3 ♗xc3+ 11.bxc3 d6 12.0-0 dxe5 13.♘xe5 ♗e6 (not 13...♗d7?? 14.♕xf7+) 14.♕c2. And even here White has the upper hand, thanks to the center pawn duo's mobility, the two bishops, and his pieces' activity.

8.cxd4

8.0-0!?± is an alternative worth examining: 8...♘gxe5 9.♘xe5 ♘xe5 10.cxd4 c6 11.♗e2 ♕h4 (else Black is simply a piece down) 12.♗e3 ♗b6 13.g3 ♕e4 14.♘c3 ♘f3+ 15.♔h1! ♕f5 16.d5!, when Black's pieces are poorly coordinated.

8...♗b4+?

The decisive mistake; on the other hand, this was not easy to foresee. 8...♘xd4!? 9.♘xd4 ♕h4 (here was Black's chance – which is why White would have been better off castling on move 8) 10.g3 ♕h3, with a complex game.

9.♔f1

Alternatively. there is the simpler 9.♘c3 d6 10.h3 ♘h6 11.♗xh6 ♗xc3+ 12.bxc3 gxh6 13.0-0±.

9...♗e7

The threat was simply 10.♗xc6.

10.h3 ♘h6 11.♗xh6

One could of course continue playing; but Black's position is hopeless. After Black recaptures, White simply sweeps all of the black forces away with d4-d5!.

1-0

29. Elshad – Masvebiashvili

August 1999

1.c3 e5 2.♕a4 ♘f6 3.e4 ♘c6

3...♗c5.

4.♘f3 ♗c5 5.♗b5 0-0 6.d4 exd4

We might consider this a theoretical position, with good reason.

7.e5

7.cxd4 is also interesting. Or even 7.0-0. For example:

7.cxd4!? ♗b4+ 8.♗d2 ♗xd2+ 9.♘bxd2 ♖e8 10.0-0 ♘xe4 11.♘xe4 ♖xe4 12.♕c2 ♖e8 13.♖fe1 h6 14.♖xe8+ ♕xe8 15.♖e1 ♕d8 16.♕e4 d5 17.♕e8+ ♕xe8 18.♖xe8+ ♔h7 19.♖f8 f6 20.♗d3+ g6 21.♖xf6 ♗g4 22.♘e5 ♘xe5 23.dxe5 ♖g8 24.f4, and White had a decisive endgame advantage in Nemtsev–Sergeev, Internet 2016.

7.0-0!? dxc3 (7...♘xe4 8.cxd4 ♗b6 9.d5 ♘c5 10.♕a3 ♘e7 11.b4 ♘e4 12.♗d3 ♘f6 13.d6 cxd6 14.♗g5 ♘ed5 15.♘c3 ♘xc3 16.♕xc3, and White has a powerful attack) 8.e5 cxb2 9.♗xb2 ♘e8 10.♘c3 ♘e7 11.♕h4, with total compensation for White. The activity of his pieces is impressive.

7...♖e8 8.cxd4 ♗b4+

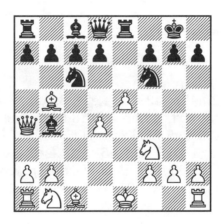

9.♔f1

9.♗d2 ♗xd2 10.♘bxd2 a6 11.0-0 ♘d5=; 9.♘c3! ♗xc3+ 10.bxc3 d6 11.0-0 dxe5 12.dxe5 ♘xe5 13.♗xe8 ♘xf3+ 14.gxf3 ♕xe8 15.♕xe8+

♘xe8 16.♗f4 and, despite his somewhat weak pawns, White has a clear advantage in the ending.

9...♘d5 10.♕b3 ♘a5?

10...♘ce7? 11.♘c3 c6 12.♗c4 ♗xc3 (12...♘xc3? 13.♗xf7+ ♔h8 14.bxc3 ♗a5 15.♘g5) 13.bxc3 b5 14.♗d3 d6 15.♕c2:

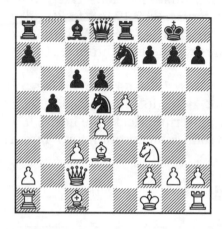

15...g6 16.h4, with attack.

11.♕xd5

11.♕c2!? h6 12.h4! c6 13.♗e2 ♗e7 (13...d6 14.a3±) 14.♕e4 d6 15.♘g5 g6 16.♘xf7 ♔xf7 17.h5 ♗f5 18.hxg6 ♗xg6 19.♗h5 ♗xh5 20.e6 ♔g7 21.♖xh5 ♗g5 22.♗xg5 hxg5 23.♕h7+ ♔f8 24.♕f7#; or 15...♗xg5 16.hxg5 dxe5 17.dxe5 c5 18.♘c3 ♘xc3 19.bxc3 ♘c6 20.f4±; finally, 15...hxg5 16.hxg5 f5 17.exf6 *e.p.* ♗xf6 18.♕h7+ ♔f8 19.♕h8+ ♔e7 20.gxf6+ ♔d7 21.♕xg7+ ♘e7 22.♖h7 ♔c7 23.fxe7 ♕d7 24.b4+−.

11...c6 12.♕e4 cxb5

12...d5!? 13.♕d3 cxb5 14.♘g5 g6 15.h4 ♗f5 16.♕f3, with attack.

13.♘g5 g6 14.♕d5 ♕e7 15.a3

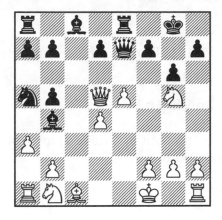

1-0

30. Nemtsev_Igor (2714) – 2000krosh (3017)

22 February 2015

1.c3 e5 2.♕a4 ♘c6 3.g4 d5 4.h3 ♘f6 5.♗g2 ♗d7

This game was played on "Chess Planet." To judge from their ratings, both players were fairly strong. Nevertheless, Black played the bishop to d7, thinking that this threatens White's queen, but we already know that this isn't so.

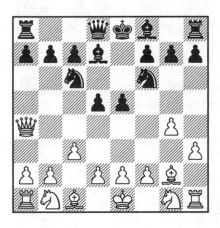

6.d3

6.g5 ♘h5 7.♗xd5 ♕xg5 leads nowhere – the advantage is more on Black's side.

6...h6 7.♘d2 ♗d6 8.♕b3

A concrete move, threatening to take a pawn, on either d5 or b7, and forcing Black's next move.

8...♘a5 9.♕c2

We had planned to go to c2 with our queen anyway, meanwhile, we have lured Black's knight to the edge of the board.

9...c5 10.♘f1

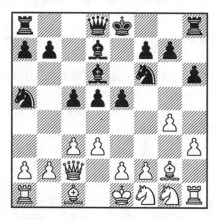

This is the most natural move for the knight: depending on the circumstances, it may go either to e3 or to g3.

Here is another good possibility for independent analysis and practice: 10.e4!? d4 11.♘e2 0-0 12.♘g3 ♗e6 13.♘f5 ♗xf5 14.exf5 ♘c6 15.♘e4, with attack.

10...♘c6 11.♘e3

In this case, the knight must go to e3. Why? Very simple: the d5-pawn is now weak (there's no pawn defending it) so White must try to make it advance to d4, in order to take over the e4 square with his knight!

11...d4 12.♘f1!

Objective achieved. Look at how our knight now goes to e4; this is an excellent post for the white pieces.

Considering that the d6-bishop is loose, there is another possibility: 12.♘c4!? ♗c7 13.♘f3 0-0 14.g5 hxg5 15.♗xg5, and the attack rolls on: the rook moves to g1, and the g7-pawn already feels its curious gaze...

12...♕c7 13.♘g3 0-0-0 14.♘e4

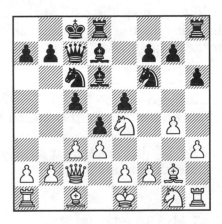

Black acts properly, getting his king away with long castling. Nonetheless, the e4 square has been occupied, and there remains but to set up White's pieces for the offensive against the queenside. Black's problem is that White doesn't plan to castle on either flank, which means that the white rooks are already in place to attack on the wings.

14...♘xe4 15.♗xe4 g6 16.a4 f5 17.♗g2!

Just so. But not to f3, where it could be vulnerable to a poke by ...e5-e4. We intend to sacrifice the g-pawn, with the strategic idea of gaining access to the e4 square for our pieces.

17...fxg4 18.a5 ♘xa5 19.hxg4 ♗xg4 20.♕a4 ♘c6

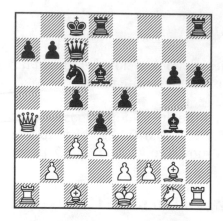

What a rich position! I chose the path of simplification, calculating that it would bring me the advantage. I advise you to delve independently into the possibilities offered by a direct attack against Black's king with b2-b4.

21.♗xc6 ♕xc6 22.♕xc6+ bxc6 23.♖xa7 ♖d7 24.♖a8+ ♗b8 25.♖xh6 ♖xh6 26.♗xh6 ♖h7 27.f3 ♗e6 28.♗d2

Here, unfortunately, I didn't see the far stronger bishop move 28.♗f8!. There are a lot of threats and the c5-pawn hangs, but mostly White threatens ♗d6.

28...♔b7 29.♖a5 ♔b6 30.c4?

30.♖a8 ♔b7 31.♖a4, with counterplay, was much better. But after all, it *is* a three-minute game: you can't expect to play all the best moves.

30...♖h1 31.♔f2 e4 32.fxe4 ♗f4

Here Black passed up a great opportunity: 32...♖h2! 33.♔f1 ♗g3∓.

33.♗xf4 ♔xa5 34.♘f3 ♖b1 35.♗d6 ♔b6 36.♘g5 ♗c8 37.e5 ♖xb2 38.e6 ♖a2 39.e7 ♗d7 40.♘e4 ♗e8 41.♘xc5 ♖a8

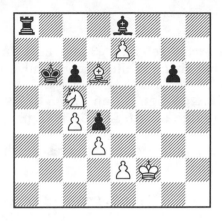

Despite being an exchange down, White is the one playing for the win. The pawn on e7 is very strong.

42.♘e6 c5

Otherwise White will play his own pawn to c5.

43.♗xc5+ ♔c6 44.♗xd4 ♔d6 45.♘g7 ♔xe7 46.♘xe8 ♔xe8 47.♗e5

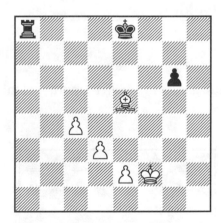

A non-standard endgame, with White having the better of it. In any event, three connected passed pawns must give him chances.

47...♔d7 48.d4 ♔e6 49.e4 ♖c8 50.c5

A trap. Saccing the rook on c5 doesn't work here, even if it might look like it draws.

50...g5

50...♖xc5?? 51.dxc5 ♔xe5 52.♔g3 and, as it turns out, the e4-pawn is untouchable, giving White a theoretically winning position.

51.♔f3 ♖g8 52.♔g4 ♖g6 53.c6 ♖g8 54.c7 ♔d7 55.d5 ♖e8 56.♔f5 g4 57.♗g3 ♖g8 58.d6 ♖e8 59.e5 ♖g8

Such pawns may not be stopped; the rest, as the cliché goes, is a matter of technique.

60.e6+ ♔c6 61.d7 ♖f8+ 62.♔e5 ♖g8 63.c8♕+ ♖xc8 64. dxc8♕+ ♔b5 65.♕c7 ♔b4 66.♔d4 ♔a4 67.♕b6 ♔a3 68.♔c3 ♔a2 69.♕b2#

My opponent played it out to mate; but this was not a sign of disrespect. It was just that, first of all, when you're playing with seconds on the clock, there's always a chance that your opponent will run out of time. And secondly, sometimes it takes so long to find the "Resigns" button on the screen that it's simpler to get mated.

31. Elshad – Tetyukhin

15 October 1979

1.c3

One of the earliest games in which the author of this system used it.

1...e5 2.♕a4

Strictly speaking, according to the classical canon such an early development of the queen should not be good. What does this teach us? And what will we teach the children? Not to bring your queen out too early, because it may come under attack from enemy pawns and pieces. How can one not remember here, in about the 'Twenties of the previous century, the Réti Opening and the Grünfeld Defense eliciting the exact same reaction from their contemporaries!

2...♘f6 3.e4 ♘c6 4.♘f3 ♗c5 5.♗b5 0-0 6.d4 exd4 7.e5 ♖e8 8.cxd4 ♗f8

8...♘xd4!?. With this move, IM Jaroslav Ulko tried successfully to alter the game's course in Elshad–Ulko, 1999. However, with exact play, White keeps the extra piece and every chance of winning: 9.♘xd4 ♖xe5+ 10.♘e2 c6 11.♗d3 d5 12.♗f4, with counterplay. However, 12.0-0!± is even stronger, as Black has no compensation for the piece.

9.0-0

One of the few lines of this system in which Elshad castles.

9...♘d5 10.♘g5!?

10.♕b3!?± is another good line: 10...♘b6 11.♘g5 d5 12.♗xc6 bxc6 13.♕c2 g6 14.♕xc6.

10.♘c3!? also deserves attention: 10...♘xc3?! 11.bxc3 a6 12.♗c4 (even 12.♖e1± is possible in connection with the pin, as Black cannot take the b5-bishop) 12...d5 (12...b5 13.♗xb5±) 13.♗d3 h6 14.h3±.

10...♕e7?

This loses, but what else should he do? 10...h6 may be the best chance: 11.♗c4 ♘ce7 (11...hxg5 12.♗xd5±). This computer defense 12.♘c3 c6 13.♗xd5 ♘xd5 14.♘ge4 ♘xc3 15.bxc3 d5 16.♘g3 produces a position with equal chances in a dynamic struggle.

11.♗c4!

11.♕c2±.

11...♘b6 12.♕c2

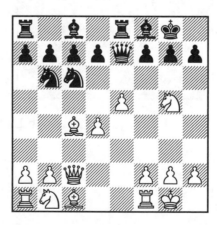

1-0

Black resigns. He cannot defend both f7 and h7.

32. Nemtsev_Igor (2844) – Brastam (2841)

16 October 2015

1.c3 e5 2.♕a4 ♘c6 3.g4 d6 4.h3 ♗d7

This was my second game against the same opponent that day (see Game 54). When Black played his bishop to d7, he was, of course, expecting my queen to retreat. But the reality is that the black knight has no good discovery square. I know this; my opponent does not. He wastes time looking for a square for the knight to jump to, gets angry...

5.♗g2 a6 6.d3 ♘ge7

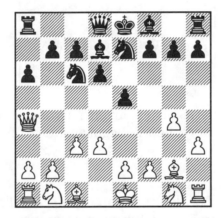

7.♘d2

White simply proceeds with his plan, which his opponent knows nothing about. Meanwhile, Black needs to resolve his main problem: developing his kingside.

7...g6 8.g5

Although this is a standard attacking move in the Elshad, there's another possibility in 8.♘e4. This is what I recommend, trying directly to exploit the weakness of Black's dark squares, i.e. 8...♗g7 9.♗g5 ♗e6 10.♘f6+ ♔f8 11.♘d5 h6 12.♘xe7 ♘xe7 13.♗xe7+ ♕xe7 14.♗xb7 ♖b8 15.♕c6.

8...♘c8 9.h4 ♘b6 10.♕c2

Too bad: White hasn't had the chance to get in h4-h5, so he can't get the queen to h4 yet. He has to drop it back to c2.

10...f6?

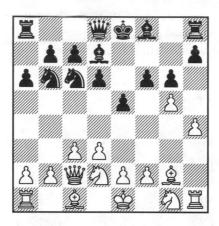

A typical error, although not an obvious one. It looks to Black as though, with this move, he will begin an attack on the white king.

11.♘f1

Perfectly good. Let's look at a pair of other excellent possibilities for White, which are even better than my move:

a) 11.♘e4! (hitting f6) 11...fxg5 (11...♗e7 12.gxf6 ♗xf6 13.♗h6) 12.hxg5 ♗g7 13.♕b3 ♕e7 14.♖xh7! (this combination was once analyzed by Elshad and me) 14...♖xh7 15.♕g8+ ♕f8 16.♕xh7;

b) 11.h5! (straightforward and strong) 11...fxg5 12.hxg6 h6 13.a4 ♕f6 14.a5 ♘c8 15.♕b3 ♖b8 16.♘e4 ♕xg6 17.♘xg5, with counterplay.

11...f5 12.a4 ♗e6 13.a5 ♘d5 14.♕a4 ♕d7 15.h5 ♗g7

A position rich in possibilities. I think I was too hasty in closing up the position. In any case, Black really would rather not capture on h5, so I should have maintained the tension, with 16.♖h4 for example.

16.h6 ♗f8 17.♘g3 ♗e7 18.e4?! ♘f4 19.♗xf4 exf4 20.♘3e2 ♗xg5 21.♘h3 ♗xh6 22.♘hxf4 ♗xf4 23.♘xf4 ♘e5??

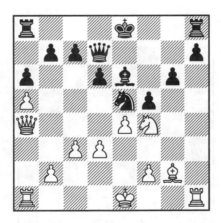

Black blinks first. He wants to trade queens, of course; but this hangs a piece, and then everything falls apart.

24.♘xe6 ♘xd3+ 25.♔d2 ♘xb2 26.♘xc7+ ♔d8 27.♕xd7+ ♔xd7 28.♘xa8 ♘c4+ 29.♔c2 ♖xa8 30.♖xh7+ ♔e6 31.exf5+ gxf5 32.♗xb7 ♖b8 33.♖e1+ ♔f6 34.f4 ♘xa5 35.♗d5 ♔g6 36.♖ee7 1-0

33. Nemtsev_Igor (2901) – FF_Hollandia (2350)

1 June 2016

1.c3 e5 2.♕a4 ♘c6 3.g4 g6 4.♗g2 ♗g7 5.d3 ♘ge7 6.h4!

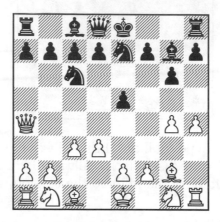

In this case, there is no need for the slower h2-h3. The way Black has played the opening, he has no choice but to castle kingside.

6...d6 7.g5

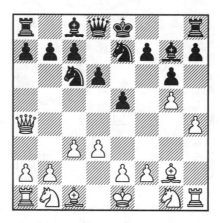

This is a typical attacking method in the Elshad. It's as if the g-pawn is holding down all three of Black's pawns on the kingside.

7.h5!? is another possible aggressive move. I recommend that you investigate both sides' possibilities here.

7...♗d7 8.♘d2

White doesn't even waste a glance on the bishop at d7. According to opening theory, Black's knight doesn't have a single good discovery square from c6. Unaware of this, Black usually searches and searches without finding any, uses up time, and then goes back to more normal moves. Which was exactly what we needed.

8...0-0 9.h5 ♘f5 10.♘e4 d5

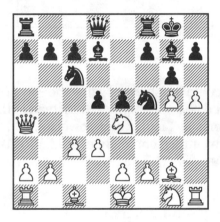

Thank you. In fact, I was planning to come down on f6 myself – and here he is, helping me go there.

11.♘f6+ ♗xf6 12.gxf6 ♕xf6 13.♗xd5

It's not so much that I have recovered my pawn; the important thing is that the dark squares around Black's king have been seriously weakened.

13...♘cd4

Black has found a knight leap after all; and he even wins the exchange, temporarily. But that won't help him.

14.♕xd7 ♘c2+ 15.♔d1 ♘xa1 16.hxg6 hxg6 17.♕xc7± ♔g7

18.♘f3

Of course, if I could finish every game the way I could find things in analysis, then I'd be a super-player!! Instead of the text, 18.♗g5!! it would have been spectacular and powerful: 18...♕xg5 19.♕xe5+ (Black doesn't have much choice here) 19...♕f6 (19...f6 only leads to mate: 20.♕c7+ ♘e7 21.♕xe7+ ♖f7 22.♕xf7#) 20.♖h7+ ♔xh7 21.♕xf6, and White is up a queen.

18...♖h8 19.♖g1 ♘h4 20.♘xe5

Here White wins simply with 20.♗g5. Or I could have just taken the knight off h4.

20...♖af8 21.♗g5 ♕f5 22.♗xh4 ♖xh4

23.♖xg6+

Not very complicated, but still a nice stroke!

23...♔h7

23...♔h8 doesn't save Black: 24.♘xf7+ ♖xf7 25.♕d8+ ♖f8 26.♕xh4+ ♕h5 27.♕xh5#. Nor does 23...♕xg6 24.♘xg6 ♔xg6 25.♕g3+ ♔h5 26.♗f3+ ♔h6 27.♕xh4+ with an extra queen: 27... ♔g7 28.♕g5+ ♔h8 29.♕f6+ ♔h7 30.♗e4+ ♔g8 31.♕h6 ♖e8 32.♗h7+ ♔h8 33.♗g6+ ♔g8 34.♕h7+ ♔f8 35.♕xf7#.

24.♖g1 ♕xf2 25.♘f3 ♖h2 26.♕xh2+ ♕xh2 27.♘xh2

How do you like that knight on a1?

1-0

34. Elshad – Bagdasarov

20 May 2015

1.c3 ♘f6 2.♕a4 e5 3.e4

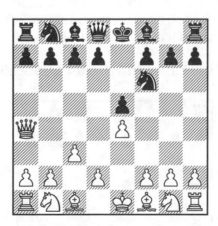

A strange transposition out of many openings.

3...♘c6 4.♘f3 ♗c5

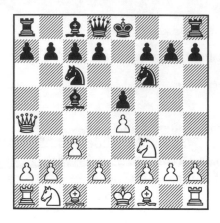

5.♗b5

This move is Elshad's patent, although this position does have many choices.

5.b4 seems convincing, given that White wins a pawn; but at the end of this variation, it's Black who has the upper hand, since he clearly holds the initiative, which outweighs the pawn: 5...♗b6 6.b5 ♘e7 7.♘xe5 d5∓.

5.d4! is the strongest move in this position. The variations are practically forced: 5...exd4 6.cxd4 ♗b4+ 7.♗d2 ♗xd2+ 8.♘bxd2 d5 9.e5 ♘e4 10.♗b5 ♘xd2 11.♗xc6+ bxc6 12.♘xd2 0-0 13.0-0±, and Black's c-file weakness will prove incurable.

5...♕e7 6.0-0 0-0 7.d4 exd4 8.cxd4 ♗b6 9.e5± ♘d5 10.♗c4!

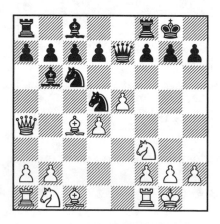

The knight falls, in what looks like a level position.

10...♘db4 11.♗g5 ♛e8 12.d5 ♘xe5 13.♛xb4 ♘xf3+ 14. gxf3 1-0

35. Elshad – Hait

Moscow

1.c3 e5 2.♛a4 ♘f6 3.e4 ♗c5 4.♘f3 ♛e7

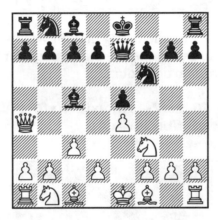

Elshad squares off against a well-known Moscow master. Black's last move would seem to prevent White's d2-d4 battering ram.

5.d4!

But of course, this is an illusion.

5...exd4 6.e5 dxc3

Otherwise, White simply recaptures the d4-pawn, gaining a large advantage without giving up any material.

7.♘xc3 0-0 8.♗e3

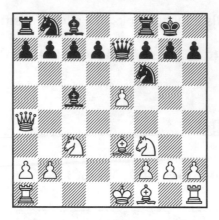

A very pretty idea. By sheltering his king against check from the black queen, White gets rid of the black knight on f6, and Black's king will be left with no defenders.

8...♗xe3 9.exf6 ♗xf2+ 10.♔xf2 ♛xf6 11.♗d3 ♛b6+ 12. ♛d4 ♛xb2+ 13.♔g3 ♛b6 14.♛e4

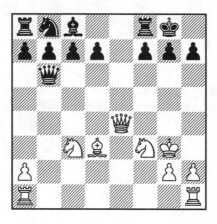

All of White's pieces are now trained upon Black's castled position. And so the second player seeks salvation in a queen trade.

14...♛g6+

14...g6.

15.♛xg6 hxg6 16.♘d5 ♘a6

Forced, in view of the threat of ♘c7.

17.♘e7+ ♚h8 18.♘g5

Very strong! The knight blocks the g-pawn, and now everything is ready for the battering ram, with h2-h4-h5xg6 followed by mate.

18...d5 19.h4 1-0

---

36. nemtsevguru (2382) – Kroket (2405)

lichess.org, 26 July 2017

1.c3 e5 2.♕a4 ♘c6 3.e4 ♘f6 4.♗b5 ♗c5 5.♘f3 0-0 6.d4 exd4 7.e5 ♖e8 8.cxd4 ♗b4+ 9.♗d2 ♗xd2+ 10.♘bxd2 ♘d5 11.0-0 a6 12.♗d3 ♘f4

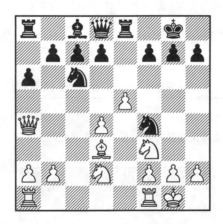

13.♗b1

13.♗e4 d5 14.exd6 ♕xd6 15.♖fe1.

13...d5 14.♕c2 ♘g6 15.a3 f6 16.♗a2

16.♖e1 fxe5 17.dxe5.

16...fxe5 17.dxe5 ♘cxe5 18.♖fe1 c6 19.♘xe5 ♖xe5 20.♘f3 ♗f5 21.♕b3 ♖xe1+ 22.♖xe1 ♕d7 23.♘d4 ♖f8 24.♕b4 h6 25.h3 ♗e4 26.f3

147

26.♖xe4.

26...♗d3 27.♕c3 ♗f5 28.♘xf5

28.g4± ♘h4 29.gxf5 ♘xf5 30.♘e6 ♖e8 31.♘f4 ♖xe1+ 32.♕xe1.

28...♕xf5 29.♗b1 ♕f6 30.♕b4 ♘e5 31.♕xb7 ♘xf3+ 32. gxf3 ♕xf3 33.♕b4 ♕g3+ 34.♔h1 ♕xh3+ 35.♔g1 ♕g3+ 36. ♔h1 c5 37.♕c3 ♕h4+ 38.♔g1 d4 39.♕d2 ♖f4 40.♖e8+ ♔f7 41.♖e2 ♖g4+ 42.♖g2 ♕h3 43.♕f2+ ♔g8 44.♖xg4

44.♗a2+ ♔h8 45.♕f8+ ♔h7 46.♕f5+ ♔h8 47.♕c8+ ♔h7 48.♗g8+ ♔g6 49.♖xg4+ ♕xg4+ 50.♕xg4+; 44.♗h7+ ♔xh7 45.♕f5+ ♔h8 46.♖xg4.

44...♕xg4+ 45.♕g2 ♕d1+ 46.♔h2

46.♕f1 ♕xf1+ 47.♔xf1 a5 48.♗g6 ♔f8 49.♔e2 c4.

46...♕xb1 47.♕d5+ ♔h8 48.♕f5 ♕xf5 49.♔g3 ♕g5+ 0-1

37. Nemtsev_Igor (2908) – cane4ka (2492)

16 August 2015

1.c3 e5 2.♕a4 ♘c6 3.g4 d5 4.h3 ♗c5

A fairly aggressive setup. We have another game in this book with a similar theme.

5.♗g2 ♗e6

As I've said many times already, this move, the bishop's development to e6 is not born out of necessity.

6.d3 ♕h4 7.d4

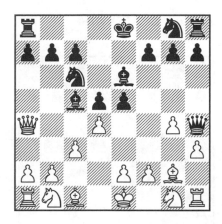

Of course, this was unexpected for Black.

7...exd4 8.♘f3

All of this is, shall we say, Elshad theory.

8...♕e7 9.b4 ♗b6 10.b5 ♘b8 11.cxd4 ♘f6 12.0-0 ♘e4 13.♗a3

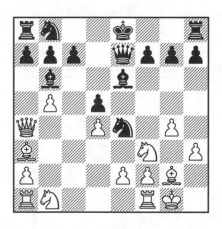

White wants to keep the black king in the center, in the spirit of the old masters. Black's reply is forced.

13...♘d6 14.♘c3 0-0 15.♖fe1 f5 16.♘e5 fxg4 17.hxg4 c6?

This is a mistake, allowing White exploit the pin to the fullest.

18.e4 dxe4 19.♘xc4 ♗c7 20.♕b4

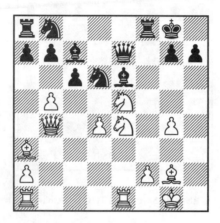

White has many attackers. Moreover, there is the additional threat of b5xc6.

20...♖d8 21.♖ac1 a5 22.bxa6 ♘xa6 23.♕xb7 ♖db8 24.♕xc6 ♖b6 25.♗xd6 ♖xc6 26.♗xe7 1-0

Already a piece down, Black resigned.

38. nemtsevguru (2382) – OrderMage (1809)

lichess.org, 6 May 2017

1.c3 e5 2.♕a4 ♘f6 3.g4 ♘c6 4.g5

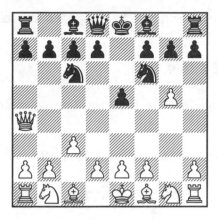

Why not? White is attacking the knight; where is it going to retreat to? In this book, you will see all possible alternatives.

4...♘d5 5.d3

A necessary move. In the first place, from c2, the bishop protects the g5-pawn; and in the second, if the knight goes to f4, then we can immediately snap it off.

5...h6 6.g6

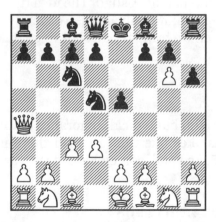

A standard pawn sacrifice. Black is practically forced to take on g6, weakening the light squares around his king.

6...fxg6 7.h4

Not giving Black the chance to straighten himself out by playing ...g6-g5.

7...♗e7 8.♗g2 ♘f6 9.♕b3

Preventing Black from castling right away, as first he must play ...d7-d5.

9...d5 10.♘d2 0-0 11.♘f1 ♔h8 12.♘e3

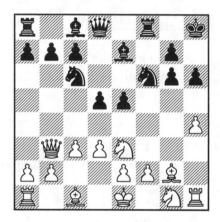

A strategic method in the Elshad. The idea runs as follows: first we attack the d5-pawn; if it advances, we simply drop our knight back to f1; and then we bring it back out to g3, taking over the e4 square.

12...♗e6

A simple oversight, but typical. Ignorance of this opening leads frequently to mistakes like this. Instead there is 12...d4 13.♘f1 ♔h7 14.♘g3 a5 15.♘e4 and, somewhere in the variations, a knight sacrifice on g5 looms.

13.♕xb7 ♕d6 14.♕b3 ♖ab8

14...d4 15.♘c4 leads nowhere.

15.♕c2 ♗g4 16.♘h3 ♕e6 17.♘g5

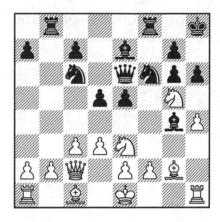

The knight reaches g5 anyway. Could Black take it? He could, but that would be awful, since it would open the h-file. So, thinks Black, let's get the king off the file first.

17...♔g8 18.♘xe6

Oops – forgot about the queen...

1-0

39. Elshad – V. Ivanov

April 1999

1.c3 e5 2.♕a4 ♘f6 3.e4 ♗c5 4.♘f3 0-0 5.d4 exd4 6.e5 ♖e8 7.cxd4 ♗b6 8.♗e2 ♘e4 9.d5

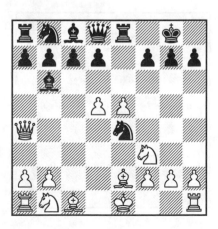

All this is part of Elshad theory. The e4-knight is attacked by the queen, so something must be done...

9...♗xf2+ 10.♔f1 f5 11.♘c3 ♘xc3 12.bxc3 ♗c5 13.♕c4 d6

Or 13...♗b6 14.d6+ ♔h8 15.♘g5.

14.♗g5 ♕d7 15.e6

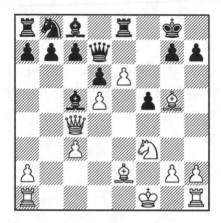

All of a sudden, the queen is trapped. He must give up the rook to save it.

15...♖xe6 16.dxe6 ♕xe6 17.♘d4 ♕xc4 18.♗xc4+ ♔h8 19.♖e1 ♗d7 20.♗d5 ♘c6 21.♗xc6 ♗xc6 22.♘xc6 bxc6 23.♔e2

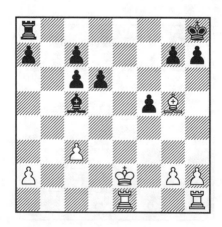

Apparently, it just now dawned on Black that he was playing down a whole rook...

1-0

40. Elshad – Myasnikov

March 1999

1.c3 e5 2.♕a4 ♘f6 3.e4 ♘c6 4.♘f3 a6 5.♗b5

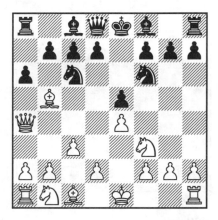

This a move you see fairly often in Elshad's games. The idea is pretty simple: to win the e5-pawn by exploiting the fact that the a6-pawn is pinned. Here we see an example of Black's attempt to refute this idea with an exchange sacrifice.

5...axb5 6.♕xa8 ♘xe4

Black does have the initiative and White's queen is in danger.

7.b4

So as to have a retreat for the queen on a3, should it become necessary (7.d4 ♘d6).

7...♘d6 8.d3 ♕f6 9.♘bd2 ♕g6 10.♘e4 ♕xg2

Not 10...♘xe4 ♕xc8+.

11.♔e2

In the spirit of the old masters, White sacrifices both rooks for mate!

11...♕xh1 12.♗g5 ♕xa1 13.♘xd6+ ♗xd6 14.♕xc8+ ♘d8 15.♕xd8#

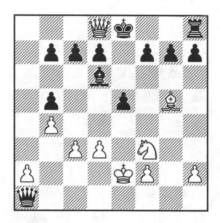

This was all forced.

41. Nemtsev_Igor (2800) – IgorPastukhov (2695)

29 May 2017

1.c3 e5 2.♕a4 ♘f6 3.e4 ♘c6 4.♗b5 ♗d6 5.♘f3 0-0 6.0-0 a6

This is seen fairly often. Black thinks that he is attacking the white bishop; the reality, however, is that his rook on a8 is hanging, so it's merely a waste of an important tempo.

7.d4 exd4

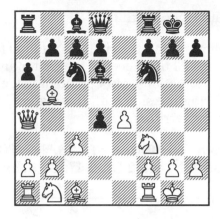

While this is merely theoretical ignorance, besides losing material. On the other hand... where should Black have learned all of this?

8.♗xc6 dxc6 9.e5

Black drops a piece. This game was played not so long ago, in 2017. Of course, I had already played dozens of blitz games in this variation; and knew how to play it. In this book, you will find a few more similar victories by White in this variation.

9...♗g4 10.exd6 ♗xf3 11.gxf3 ♘d5 12.♕xd4 f5 13.dxc7 ♕xc7 14.c4 ♘e7 15.♗f4

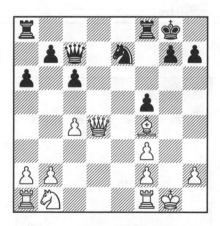

In principle, we could just draw the curtain right here. Black is missing a piece, as well as any compensation for it.

15...♕c8 16.♘c3 ♘g6 17.♖ad1

Usually in such positions, the simplest method for realizing the advantage is to bring all the pieces to the center and start offering exchanges. In such situations, our opponent will either acquiesce to the trade (favoring the side with the material advantage), or retreat, surrendering territory.

17...♔h8 18.♔h1 c5 19.♕d6 ♖f6 20.♕c7 ♕f8 21.♘d5 ♖c8 22.♕xb7 ♖e6 23.♖fe1 ♖ec6 24.♗e5 ♕d8 25.♕xg7#

42. Papin – Vojevodin

1.c3 e5 2.♕a4 ♘f6 3.g4

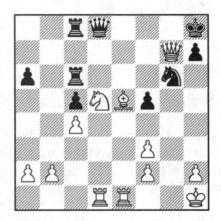

In this game, besides the game move, there is also 3.e4. Identical games are analyzed in detail elsewhere in the book.

3...h6

A natural reaction. It should be said that Black is a very strong master from Moscow, who didn't resolve the problems set for him.

4.d3 ♘c6 5.♗g2 d5 6.g5

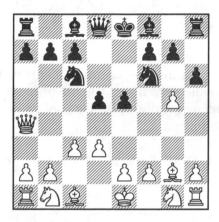

Yet another typical move in this opening, opening the g-file, both for the attack and for the pin.

6...hxg5 7.♗xg5 ♗e7 8.♘f3 ♗e6?

A blunder – which is pretty typical.

9.♘xe5 0-0 10.♘xc6 bxc6 11.♕xc6 1-0

43. Elshad – Vojevodin

1999

1.c3 e5 2.♕a4 ♘f6 3.e4 ♘c6 4.♘f3 d6 5.d4 ♗d7 6.dxe5 ♘xe5 7.♕c2 ♘xf3+ 8.gxf3

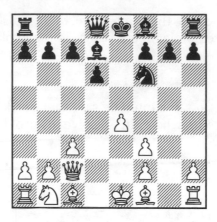

A position which is non-standard to the utmost degree. What's Black going to do? On the one hand, it seems as though White's doubled pawns would give Black the advantage. But in fact, the g-file has been opened up for White's rook, so castling kingside certainly isn't safe for Black.

8...♗c6 9.♗e3 d5 10.♘d2 ♕e7 11.0-0-0 a6 12.♘b3 dxe4 13.♘a5

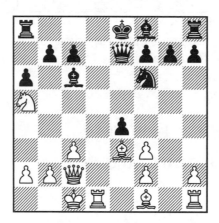

Playing blitz is very difficult when you don't have even a single marker to guide your play. He doesn't want to trade off the bishop. Black has simply lost his feel for the board.

13...♗d5 14.c4 ♕b4 15.♗d2 1-0

44. Elshad – Gerasimov

1999

1.c3 e5 2.♕a4 ♘f6 3.e4 ♘c6 4.♘f3 d6 5.d4 ♗d7 6.dxe5 ♘xe5 7.♕c2 ♘xf3+ 8.gxf3 ♗c6 9.♗e3

We also find this variation in Elshad's game against Vojevodin, above.

9...a5

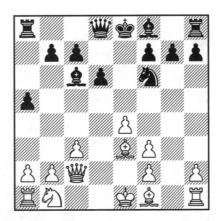

10.♘d2 ♗e7 11.♗d3 g6 12.h4 ♘h5 13.0-0-0 ♗xh4

Very brave. I compare these kinds of positions to driving on the turnpike. Let's say that I need to get somewhere quickly. There's a level, open road (the h-file), but it has a barrier laid across it (the pawn on h4). We get an offer to open the barrier for a meager piece of silver (that h4-pawn), and to go swiftly on a good road, right down to Black's king! Well, of course we're going to hand over that little piece of silver!

14.f4

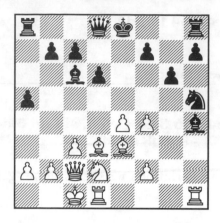

Naturally, it would have been even better for White if the black king had already castled short; but here too, danger awaits at every turn.

14...♗e7 15.♗f1 f5

Astonishingly careless, "feasting in a time of plague." To open up his king like this – and for what, exactly? To win another pawn?

16.♗c4 ♘g7 17.♗d4 ♔f8 18.exf5 ♗xh1 19.♖xh1

Well, that's good: it's an exchange. Now look at the rest of the pieces – and at the black king. Who wants to play Black's side here?

19...♗f6 20.fxg6 h5 21.♘e4 ♗xd4 22.cxd4 d5 23.♘g5 dxc4

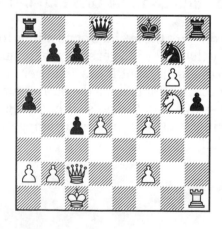

I have to say that Elshad's attack is wonderful! Already down a rook, now White sacs the knight!

24.♘e6+ ♘xe6 25.♕f5+ ♔e7 26.♖e1 ♕d7 27.d5 ♔d8 28.dxe6 ♕e7 29.♖d1+ ♔e8 30.♖d7

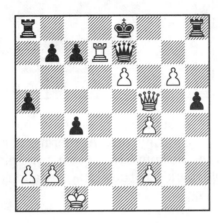

Concerning this position, one would like to ask: what are Black's two rooks doing here?

1-0

45. Elshad – Dragomaretsky

1999

1.c3 e5 2.♕a4 ♘f6 3.e4 ♘c6 4.♘f3 ♗c5 5.♗b5 ♕e7 6.0-0 0-0 7.d4 exd4 8.cxd4 ♗b6 9.e5 ♘e8 10.♘c3 a6 11.♘d5 ♕d8 12.♗d3

I can safely state that this is a theoretical position. Once again, a well-known international master has failed to cope with the problems posed by the Elshad Opening.

12...h6 13.♘xb6 cxb6 14.d5 ♘b8

What can we say! All of Black's pieces have undeveloped back to the eighth rank. White's army, on the other hand, is fully deployed and aiming wholly at the kingside. A basic principle of chess holds that, when you hold this kind of advantage, you must seek to attack.

15.♗xh6 gxh6

If Black declines the piece, then White will enjoy both a material and an enormous positional advantage.

16.♕e4 f5 17.exf6 ♘xf6 18.♕g6+ ♔h8 19.♕xh6+ ♔g8 20.♕g6+ ♔h8 21.d6

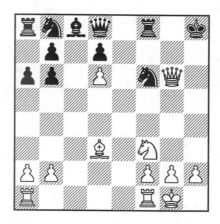

Very nice! A single pawn ties up Black's whole queenside.

21...♕e8 22.♕h6+ ♔g8 23.♖ae1 ♕f7 24.♘g5 ♕g7 25.♗c4+

And here's still another consequence of advancing White's d-pawn: the opening of a vital diagonal for the bishop.

25...♖f7 26.♗xf7+ ♕xf7 27.♖e7 ♕f8 28.♕g6+ ♔h8 29.♖h7+ ♘xh7 30.♕xh7#

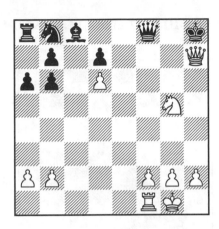

Note that Black was hardly a novice who doesn't even know how the pieces move!

46. Nemtsev_Igor (2903) – vsim (2533)

1 June 2016

1.c3 ♘f6 2.♕a4 ♘c6 3.g4 h6 4.♗g2 e5 5.d3 a6 6.h3 b5 7. ♕c2 ♗b7 8.♔f1

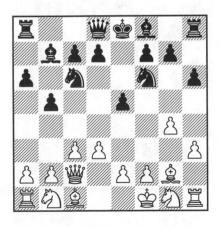

Black has handled the opening fairly well, and now I have correctly moved my king to f1, since there was the threat of jumping to d4 with the black knight and winning my g2-bishop. On the other hand, this king move still fits into White's scheme, one that Elshad himself loves to implement.

8...♗c5 9.♘d2 d6 10.♘e4 ♘xe4 11.♗xe4 0-0 12.h4 ♘a5

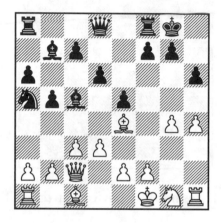

13.♗xb7

An automatic capture: 13.b4 would have won a piece.

13...♘xb7 14.g5 h5 15.♘f3 f5?

16.gxf6

As a rule, one should usually play this in similar situations. But there was also a better possibility in this specific case: 16.b4 ♗b6 17.♕b3+ ♔h8 18.g6 f4 19.♖g1±. The threat of ♖g5-h5 speaks loudly.

16...♕xf6 17.♖g1 d5 18.♕b3 c6 19.♖g5 ♘a5 20.♕c2 ♖ae8 21.b4

White wins a piece anyway; the compensation for it is clearly insufficient.

21...♗xf2 22.♔xf2 e4 23.dxe4 dxe4 24.bxa5 exf3 25. ♕b3+ ♔h7 26.♖xh5+ ♔g6 27.♖g5+ ♔h7 28.♕c2+ ♔g8 29.e4 ♕d6

30.♖g3

Black's attack comes to an end even before it started. Not 30.e5? ♖xe5 31.♗e3 ♖xg5 32.♕b3+ ♖d5 33.c4 bxc4 34.♕xc4 ♕h2+ 35.♔f1 ♕h1+ 36.♔f2 ♕xa1.

30...♕e7 31.♗g5 ♕xe4 32.♕xe4 ♖xe4 33.♖xf3 1-0

Chapter 3

//

Black Plays ...g7-g6, King's Indian Style

47. Nemtsev_Igor (2777) – aptor2009 (2829)

8 October 2016

1.c3 g6

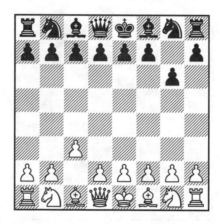

Here we have a fairly common way of answering this opening, especially for those who love the King's Indian or Grünfeld Defenses, but who are unfamiliar with the Elshad System. The trouble is that the g6-pawn becomes the focus of an attack on the king. In this sense, any fianchetto is a happy development for Elshad fans! Incidentally, fianchettoing the bishop to g7 against the pawn on c3 cannot be considered a wise course of action. See, for example, Ulf Andersson's games with White in the Anti-Grünfeld.

2.♕a4 ♗g7

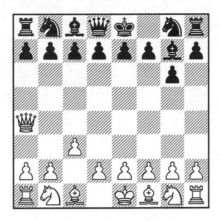

3.h4

Since a direct attack on the black king is part of White's plan, there is no point in deviating from this scheme. Specifically, there's no need to play g2-g4 and h2-h3, and only then h4-h5. Other nuances of the attack, you will soon learn about.

3...♘f6 4.g4 c6

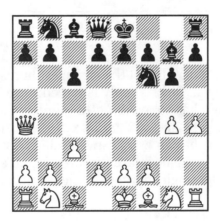

5.h5

All strong and logical. But there is also another – and I'm not afraid to use this word – classical way to carry out the attack in this opening:

5.g5 ♘h5. Black often replies this way, because he doesn't know what White is up to. As in the Yugoslav Attack of the Sicilian Dragon, Black considers that on h5 his knight will block White's attack. There follows 6.♗g2 0-0 7.♗f3. What a surprise! I myself once fell for this, playing against Elshad himself. 7...d6 8.♗xh5 gxh5 9.d3 ♘d7 10.♘d2 e5 11.♘f1 ♕e7 12.♘g3. One might say that Black has been knee-capped.

5...d5 6.h6 ♗f8 7.g5 ♘e4 8.d3 ♘c5

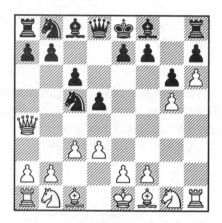

9.♕c2

A standard solution, but not the strongest here. 9.♕d4±! is how I should have played. Black's reply is forced: 9...e5 10.♕xe5+ ♕e7 11.♕g3 (White just has to avoid getting greedy: 11.♕xh8 ♘xd3+ 12.♔d1 ♘xf2+ 13.♔e1 ♘xh1∓; 12.♔d2 ♕xg5+) 11...♗f5 12.♗e3. White is clearly better: he has an extra pawn and is playing in the spirit of Elshad's Opening. Black is already sweating. It's like he's lost in the forest without a single marker to orient himself by.

9...e5 10.♗g2 ♗e7 11.♘f3 e4 12.dxe4

You *must* play this move!

12...dxe4

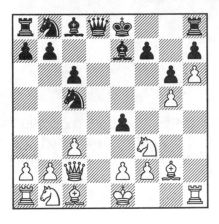

13.♘e5

13.♘d4 is better. The variation runs as follows: (13.♘d4) 13...
♗xg5 14.♗xg5 ♕xg5 15.♗xe4 ♘xe4 16.♕xe4+ ♕e7 17.♘d2 ♕xe4
18.♘xe4 0-0 19.♖g1±. This is a very strong move, keeping the black
bishop from coming out to f5. White is clearly on top. The pawn
on h6 creates a precondition for mate on the eighth rank, and the
gaping holes on the dark squares are tailor-made for the white
knights. This is but a short listing of Black's woes. And, well, at
the moment, as a rule, Black is already experiencing a severe time
deficit, and self-doubt as well.

13...♗xg5 14.♘d2 f5 15.b4 ♘cd7

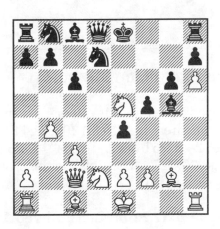

16.♘xe4!

Excellent!

16...♘xe5

Or 16...fxe4 17.♕xe4 ♕e7 18.♗xg5 ♕xe5 19.♖h4! (after a move like this, anyone's head would be spinning!) 19...♕xe4 20.♖xe4+ ♔f8 21.0-0-0. Black's position is hopeless: *Stockfish* has it at +9 in White's favor.

17.♘xg5

17.♗xg5+− is of course far stronger: 17...♕c7 18.♘f6+ ♔f7 19.0-0-0 a5 20.e4 axb4 21.cxb4 ♗e6 22.exf5 gxf5 23.♖he1 ♖xa2 24.♕c3 ♘g6 25.♘d7 ♘xd7 26.♕g7+ ♔e8 27.♖xe6+ ♘e7 28.♕xe7#.

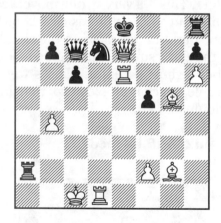

17...♘a6 18.♗f4 ♕e7 19.♖d1 ♗d7 20.♔f1

20.♖h3!. (The rook goes up one "floor" – a maneuver typical for this opening. The threat is 21.♖e3.) 20...♘g4 21.b5 ♘c5 22.♕d2 ♘e6 23.♘xe6 ♗xe6 24.bxc6 bxc6 25.♗xc6+ ♔f7 26.♗d6 ♕f6 27.♖b1 ♖ad8 28.♖b7+ ♔g8 29.♖g7+. The finish is the crowning touch, as our predecessors used to say.

20...♘f7 21.♘xf7 ♕xf7 22.b5 ♘c5 23.bxc6 ♗xc6 24.♗xc6+ bxc6

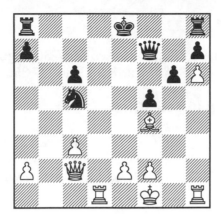

25.♕b2

The rook lift 25.♖h3! wins: 25...♘e4 26.♖hd3 0-0 27.♖d7.

Here, I would like to touch on the chess classics, and talk about open lines for the rooks. By itself, an open line doesn't mean a lot; much more important is whether there are invasion squares available at the end of it. In other words, an open file for the rook is a "working road" and the seventh rank is its workplace.

27...♕f6 28.♖g7+ ♔h8 29.♖dd7+−.

25...0-0 26.c4 ♘e4 27.f3 ♘f6

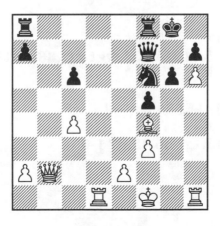

28.♖g1

28.♖d6 (stronger) 28...c5 29.♗e5 ♘d7 30.♖xg6+ hxg6 31.h7+ ♕xh7 32.♖xh7 ♔xh7 33.♕b7 ♖ad8 34.♗d6 ♖f7 35.♕d5+−.

28...♖fe8 29.♖d6 ♖e6 30.c5

Embarrassingly, I didn't see 30.♖xe6 ♕xe6 31.♕b7+−.

30...♖ae8 31.♖g2 ♘d5 32.♗d2 ♖xd6 33.cxd6 ♕d7 34.♕d4 ♖e6

35.e4!

The decisive breakthrough.

35...fxe4 36.fxe4 ♖f6+ 37.♔g1 ♕f7 38.exd5 ♖f1+ 39.♔h2 g5 40.♕g7+

40.♖xg5+ ♔f8 41.♕h8+ ♕g8 42.♕xg8#.

40...♕xg7 41.hxg7 h6 42.d7 1-0

48. Elshad – Morozevich

immortalchess.net, 6 May 2015

1.c3 ♘f6 2.♕a4 g6 3.g4 ♗g7 4.♗g2 0-0 5.g5

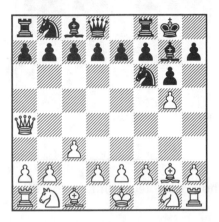

One of the *tabiyas* of this opening – and played not against some beginner, but against the super-grandmaster Alexander Morozevich in a rapid chess tournament.

Black's knight can't go to h5 for the time being. Note, too, that White's queen will now try to move over to the kingside. Generally speaking, the fianchetto isn't such a good idea against the Elshad Opening, as there is a prime target for White's attack – namely, the g6-pawn.

5...♘e8

It's certainly a good idea to show the reader how to play against the knight's escape to h5. This is quite often played, especially in blitz or rapid games, because the player of Black is unaware of how White will respond to it. After 5...♘h5, White simply replies 6.♗f3! d5 7.♗xh5 gxh5 8.♕h4 ♗f5 9.d3 c6 10.♘d2 ♘d7 11.♘f1 ♗g6 12.♘g3 e5 13.♘xh5, with a clear advantage.

6.h4 e5 7.d3 d5 8.h5±

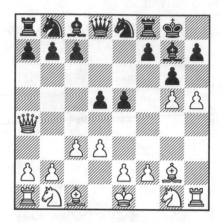

The engines show a stable advantage for White.

8...d4!

Forced. Of course, the grandmaster recognizes White's chief threat, which is shifting the queen to h4. Let's see what happens if Black overlooks the idea of transferring the queen:

8...♘c6? 9.♕h4! (9.hxg6 fxg6 10.♕h4 ♗e6 11.♕xh7+ ♔f7 12.♖h6 ♗f5 13.e4 dxe4 14.dxe4 ♖h8 15.exf5 ♖xh7 16.♖xh7 ♔g8 17.fxg6) 9...♕d6 10.hxg6 fxg6 11.b3 ♘e7 12.♗a3 c5 13.♕xh7+ ♔f7 14.♘d2 ♖h8 15.♕xh8 ♗xh8 16.♖xh8 ♗e6 17.♘gf3 ♔g7 18.♖h2 ♘c6 19.0-0-0. In this non-standard position, White has a powerful attack. I have often seen how Elshad has left Black's position in a shambles. In this opening, the material balance doesn't count for much.

9.hxg6 hxg6 10.♘f3

10.cxd4!?. Take a look also at this turn of events. (All these ideas are Elshad's.) After 10...exd4:

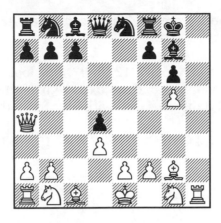

...there could follow 11.♗f4 ♘c6 12.♘d2 ♗f5 13.♗xc6! bxc6 14.♕xc6 ♖b8 15.♘b3 ♗e6 16.♘f3 ♗xb3 17.axb3 ♖xb3 18.♗e5 ♗xe5 19.♘xe5 ♖xb2 20.♘xf7 ♖xf7 21.♕xg6+ ♘g7 22.♕h6 ♔f8 23.g6+−.

10...♘c6 11.♘bd2 ♘d6

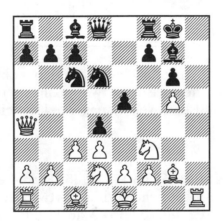

12.♘h4

Making way for the g2-bishop and threatening various combinations, such as 13.♘xg6 fxg6 14.♗d5+.

12.c4!?. My favorite move in such positions! The game stabilizes – the e4 square is in our possession. But Elshad himself prefers to leave the pawn on c3 so that his queen may, if the occasion arises, deliver a fatal check from b3. There can follow 12...a5 13.a3 ♗d7 14.c5 ♘f5 15.♘e4.

Another unorthodox idea is 12.♖h4!?. Just look at this: 12...♗d7 13.♕c2 ♖e8 14.♘e4 ♘xe4 15.dxe4 dxc3 16.bxc3 ♕e7 17.♗e3 ♖ad8 18.♖b1 b6 19.♗h3 ♗xh3 20.♖xh3, with play for both sides.

12...♗g4 13.♘e4 ♘xe4 14.♗xe4 ♕d7 15.♕b3 ♘a5

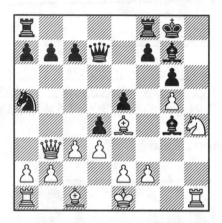

The climax of the struggle. Black's position is objectively lost. It looks like only the difference in the two opponents' playing strength begins to tell; and Elshad even manages to lose this one.

16.♕a3

16.♕b4!? wins after 16...b6 17.f3 ♗h5 18.cxd4 exd4 19.♘g2 c5 20.♕d2 ♖ad8 21.♘f4 ♘c6, when White has two ways to bring home the full point: 22.♘d5! ♕d6 23.♘f6+ ♗xf6 24.gxf6 ♕xf6 25.♕h6 ♕g7 26.♗xc6+−; and 22.♘xh5 gxh5 23.♖xh5+−.

16...b6 17.cxd4

17.b4!± should also lead to an easy win: 17...♘c6 18.♕a4.

17...exd4 18.b4 ♘c6 19.♕a4 ♘e5 20.♕xd7 ♗xd7 21.♗xa8 ♖xa8 22.♗f4

22.♗d2±.

22...a5 23.bxa5 ♖xa5

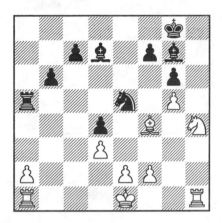

The game's further course could not be reconstructed. White was a healthy exchange to the good. Elshad himself said that, at some point, he blundered material. However, this does not lessen our enthusiasm in playing over the game. One of the world's strongest grandmasters was thoroughly outplayed. Bravo!

The story of this game had a sequel. A few days later, Morozevich flew off to play on a team – apparently, the Russian championship. In the morning, over breakfast, he related the following story; Maksim Notkin was sitting at the table. "I was playing this game," said Morozevich, "a rapid game against some amateur; and every move I made was the strongest one in the position, but my position kept getting worse and worse. I don't understand how this could happen."

That's how he described this game.

1-0

49. Elshad – Petrosian

1.c3 ♘f6 2.♕a4 g6 3.g4 ♗g7 4.d3 0-0

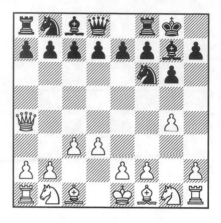

5.g5

Strongest!

5...♘d5 6.h4 ♘b6

Black wants to get his vulnerable knight out of the center as fast as possible to a well-supported position. However, more important is the fact that the knight has abandoned its king.

7.♕f4 e5 8.♕h2 f6?

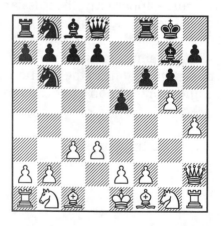

V. Tsarev, a chess master, made the same kind of mistake (see Game 51); now it's another master who shares a World Champion's name.

9.♘f3

Simple and strong. Moving the bishop out to g2, as in Elshad's game against Tsarev, wouldn't make any sense here, since he wouldn't be able to get to the d5 square.

The direct attack would also be very strong, i.e. 9.h5!? fxg5 (9...♕e8 also fails to save Black: 10.hxg6 ♕xg6 11.gxf6 ♖xf6 12.♘f3 ♘c6 13.♖g1 ♕f7 14.♘g5 ♕g6 15.♘e4 ♕f7 16.♘xf6+ [one gets the impression that the single developed white piece – the knight – has destroyed the whole black army] 16...♕xf6 17.♗h6 d5 18.♖xg7+ ♕xg7 19.♗xg7 ♔xg7 20.♘d2) 10.hxg6 h6 11.♘h3 ♖f5 (a capture on g5 was threatened) 12.e4 ♖f4 (an exchange sacrifice, totally in the spirit of Petrosian the Great – but...) 13.♘xf4 exf4 14.♗xf4 gxf4 15.♕xf4 d5 16.♕f7+ ♔h8 17.♖xh6+ ♗xh6 18.♕h7#:

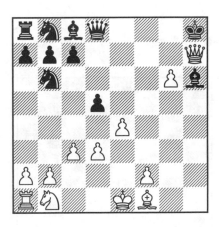

9...♘c6 10.h5 f5

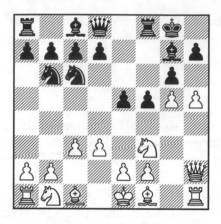

11.hxg6 hxg6 12.♕h7+ ♔f7 13.♖h6

Notice the rook's participation. White has a winning game.

13...♘e7

13...♖g8 14.♖xg6 ♔f8 15.♖f6+ ♗xf6 16.gxf6 ♕xf6 17.♗h6+ ♖g7
18.♘g5 ♔e8 19.♗xg7 ♕xg5 20.♘d2 d6 21.♘f3 ♕e7 22.♕g8+ ♔d7
23.♗h3+−.

14.♘xe5+ ♔e6 15.♕xg7

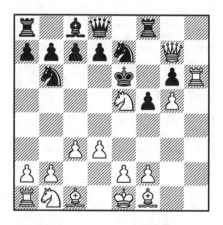

About this game, we have to ask: which one was, in fact, in the greater danger – White's uncastled king or Black's securely protected monarch?

1-0

---

50. Elshad – Savenko

1.c3 ♘f6 2.♕a4 g6 3.g4 ♗g7 4.♗g2 c6

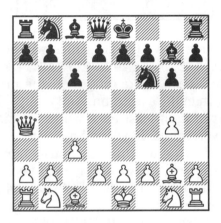

5.d3

We can call this a theoretical line in the Elshad Opening. The idea behind it runs as follows: the fourth rank remains clear in order to facilitate the free movement of White's queen along it. The f4 square is taken under the control of White's dark-squared bishop so that, after g4-g5 and ...♘f6-h5, this knight can't jump to f4, since sometimes Black manages to guess that he can first drive the white queen back to c2. The d-pawn's move also opens the route b1-d2-f1-g3 for the queen's knight to reach the kingside.

5.g5!?. Why not play this right away? It looks like a good move: 5...♘d5 (5...♘h5 6.♗f3 d5 7.♗xh5 gxh5 8.♕h4 e5 9.♕xh5 ♕e7 with compensation; 5...b5 6.♕h4 ♘h5 7.d3 0-0 8.♗f3 d5 9.♗xh5 gxh5 10.♘d2 ♘d7 11.♘f1 e5 12.♘g3 ♖e8 13.♘xh5±) 6.d3 0-0 7.h4! ♘b6 (Black hasn't guessed yet where the white queen is headed) 8.♕f4 e5 9.♕h2! d5 10.h5:

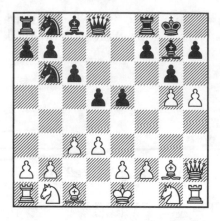

10...♗f5 (expecting only 11.hxg6, which will be answered with 11...♗xg6) 11.e4 dxe4 12.dxe4 ♗g4 13.♗f3 ♗xf3 14.♘xf3 ♖e8 15.♗e3. Notice that White doesn't take on g6, on the principle that the threat is stronger than the execution. And really – let's keep Black constantly in fear of it, at least for a while; let him spend all his time calculating variations. Black will never find a favorable moment to capture on h5, since then the house of cards that he has built around his king will collapse. Play might continue 15...♘8d7 16.hxg6 hxg6 17.♕h7+ ♔f8 18.♘bd2 ♕e7 19.♘h4 ♖ad8 20.0-0-0 ♘c5 21.♘f5 gxf5 22.exf5 f6 23.gxf6 ♕xf6 24.♗xc5+ ♔f7 25.♕h5+ ♔g8 26.♖dg1 e4 27.♖xg7+ ♔xg7 28.♕h7#:

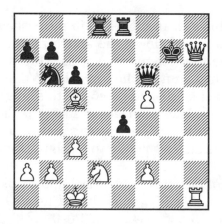

And that's that, more or less.

5...d5 6.g5 ♘fd7

Compared to variations where a black pawn is still on d7, Black now has this retreat for his knight. In any case, all of Black's pieces have now left the kingside.

7.h4 ♘b6

8.♕b4

If you were to set up the diagram position as an exercise to guess White's next move, I doubt that this move would be first on the list. Let me try to explain the idea behind it. Generally speaking, White's queen wants to go to f4, and from there to h2. But when the lady gets to f4, she could be driven off by ...e7-e5. Look at the game, and you'll see that Elshad reserved e5 specially for Black's bishop.

8.♕f4!? (this move was, of course, both possible and strong) 8...e5 9.♕g3 0-0 10.h5, with attack.

8...♘8d7 9.h5 ♘f8

10.h6

This is what Elshad was aiming for. A genius idea!

10.♘f3 would lead to a complex battle – which, on the other hand, usually happens in Elshad's Opening anyway: 10...gxh5 11.♖xh5 ♘bd7 12.♗e3 ♘g6 13.♘bd2, with play for both sides.

10...♗e5 11.♘f3 ♗d6 12.♕d4 ♖g8??

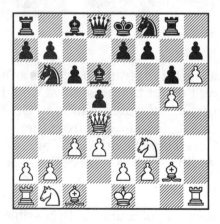

Naturally, Black didn't want to give up a pawn with ...e7-e5.

13.♕g7

What a shock! The rook is gone!

1-0

51. Elshad – Tsarev

Chess.com, 2 October 2015

1.c3 ♘f6 2.♕a4 g6 3.g4 ♗g7 4.♗g2 0-0 5.g5 ♘e8 6.h4 e5 7.d3

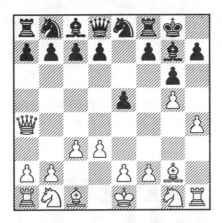

7...f6??

We saw all of this in Elshad–Morozevich. Elshad's opponent in this game was the very well-known master, Valery Tsarev. He was a very strong blitz player – in his day, rumor had it that he played as strongly as did Valentin Arbakov. But here he goes down. And this, after what seemed like a logical opening-up of the game (7...d5 8.h5 d4).

8.♗d5+ ♔h8

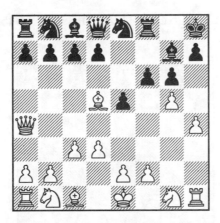

8...♖f7. A sad alternative. Meanwhile, White can pick up the exchange and continue the attack: 9.h5 c6 10.hxg6 hxg6 11.♗xf7+

187

♚xf7 12.gxf6 ♝xf6 13.f4+−. This portrait, as the expression goes, was painted with oils!

9.h5

Black can't defend against all the threats. Besides the direct pawn captures, White also threatens to bring his queen to h4.

9...fxg5

Enjoy the pretty mates at the end of each variation. They are the sort of mates that will make your hair fall out! (I've tried it myself, alas.)

9...gxh5 10.♖xh5 f5 11.♕h4 h6 12.♖xh6+ ♝xh6 13.♕xh6#:

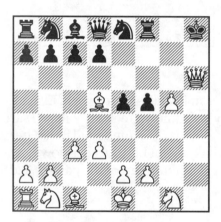

Or this: 9...c6 10.hxg6 cxd5 11.♕h4 h6 12.gxh6 f5 13.hxg7+ ♚xg7 14.♕h6+ ♚g8 15.♕h8#:

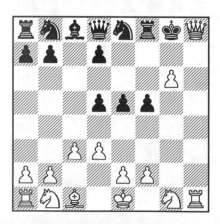

10.hxg6 h6

10...♘f6 doesn't save Black, either; at the end of this variation, the mate is, as always, a cute one: 11.♗xg5 ♕e8 12.♗xf6 ♖xf6 13.♖xh7#:

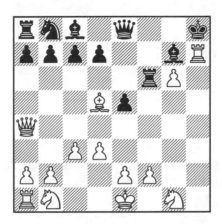

11.♘f3 ♕f6

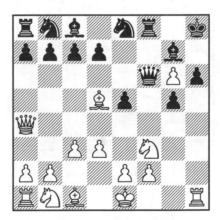

11...♖xf3. This is a chance, but hardly constitutes salvation. Follow this line through mate: 12.exf3 ♘c6 13.♘a3 d6 14.♗xc6 bxc6 15.♗xg5 ♕xg5 16.♕xc6 ♖b8 17.♕xe8+ ♗f8 18.♕xf8#:

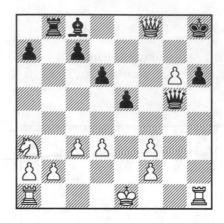

12.♗f7

12.♕g4. Here's another way to mate Black: 12...♕xg6 13.♘h4 ♕h7 14.♕xg5 hxg5 15.♘g6#:

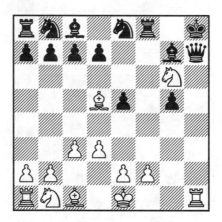

Very nice!

12...♘d6

12...♖xf7. Could this have been a better way, sacrificing the exchange? Let's enjoy yet another beautiful checkmate: 13.gxf7 ♕xf7 14.♗xg5 d5 15.♗xh6 ♗f6 16.♘xe5 ♗xe5 17.♗f4+ ♔g8 18.♗xe5 ♘c6 19.♖h8#:

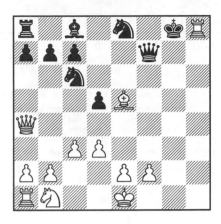

13.♗xg5 ♛f5 14.♗xh6 ♞xf7 15.♗xg7+

Or 15.gxf7. How would you like a variation with mate at the end of it, e.g. 15...♗xh6 16.♖xh6+ ♔g7 17.♕h4 ♔xf7 18.♖h7+ ♔e8 19.♕e7#:

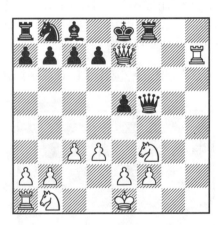

15...♔xg7 16.♖h7+ ♔xg6 17.♞h4+

The queen goes; the master resigns. A memorial to V. Tsarev: a chevalier of chess, *sans peur et sans reproche*.

1-0

52. NemtsevIgor (2154) – IvanAG (2119)

Live Chess Chess.com, 20 May 2015

1.d3

By starting a game with a move like this, we will often provoke our opponent into placing his center pawns actively on d5 and e5. This time, my opponent didn't fall for it.

1...♘f6 2.c3 g6 3.♘d2 ♗g7 4.h3 0-0 5.g4 d6 6.♗g2 h5

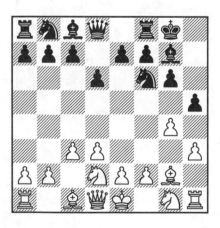

At least double-edged. At any rate, it's another pawn drifting away from his king.

7.gxh5 ♘xh5 8.♘f1 e5 9.♗f3 ♕h4

This is my very first time having this position. I think I was able to come up with an excellent idea for storming the black king.

10.♗xh5 ♕xh5 11.h4

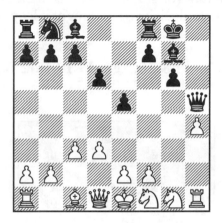

The h-pawn wants to go further; the knight will assist. Driving the queen away from the h5 square – that's pretty simple.

11...♘c6 12.♘g3 ♕g4 13.h5 ♗d7 14.♘f3 ♖ae8 15.♖h4 ♕e6

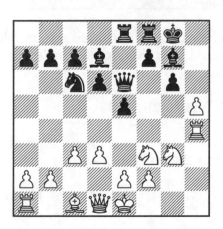

But here I did not play the best move. All the same, the basic idea was to pry open the king's pawn cover.

16.h6

Here's how White should have played: 16.♘g5! ♛e7 17.hxg6! fxg6 18.♛b3+ ♗e6 19.♛xb7 ♛d7 20.♘xe6 ♖xc6 21.♘e4± and White's advantage is close to decisive. The knight's leap to g5 is hard to prevent.

16...♗f6 17.h7+ ♚h8 18.♗g5 d5 19.♛d2 b5 20.0-0-0 a5 21.♗xf6+ ♛xf6 22.♛h6 ♛g7 23.♛g5 b4 24.♖g1

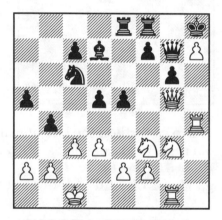

The contest is being played for three results. All of my remaining pieces have been transferred to the king's wing, but my king is also in danger.

24...bxc3 25.♘h5 f6 26.♛g3

Better would have been to take the queen right away: 26.♛xg6 ♛xg6 27.♖xg6 cxb2+ 28.♚b1 ♘e7 29.♖xf6±.

26...cxb2+ 27.♚b1 ♛f7 28.♛xg6 ♛xg6 29.♖xg6 e4 30.dxe4 dxe4

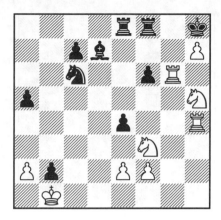

Fortunately, I found a combination that transposes to an endgame giving White a minimal advantage.

31.♖g8+ ♖xg8 32.hxg8♕+ ♖xg8 33.♘xf6+ ♔g7 34.♘xd7 exf3 35.exf3 ♖d8 36.♘c5 ♔g8 37.♔xb2 ♘b4 38.a3 ♘d3+ 39.♘xd3 ♖xd3 40.♖f4 ♔g7 41.♖f5 ♔g6 42.♖xa5 ♖xf3 43.♖c5 ♖xf2+ 44.♔b3 ♖f7 45.♔b4

This ending is not as simple as it looks. White has an outside passed pawn, and the black pieces are too far away.

45...♔f6 46.♔b5 ♔e6 47.♔c6 ♖e7??

The losing mistake.

48.a4

As it turns out, now the a-pawn cannot be stopped.

48...♖h7 49.a5 ♖g7 50.a6 ♖g8 51.♔xc7 ♖g7+ 52.♔b6 ♔d6 53.♖c6+ ♔d5 54.♖c7 ♖g1 55.a7 ♖b1+ 56.♔a6 ♖a1+ 57.♔b7 ♖b1+ 58.♔c8 ♖a1 59.♔b8 ♖b1+ 60.♖b7 ♖a1 61.a8♕ ♖xa8+ 62.♔xa8

Due to the inertia of a three-minute game, my opponent kept playing until he ran out of time.

62...♔e5 63.♔b8 ♔d4 64.♔c7 ♔e4 65.♔d6 ♔f4 66.♖b4+ ♔e3 67.♔d5 ♔d2 68.♖e4 ♔c2 69.♖d4 ♔c3 70.♔c5 ♔c2 71.♖c4+ 1-0

53. I. Nemtsev – P. Stefan

Chess.com, 23 July 2016

1.c3 ♘f6 2.♕a4 g6 3.g4 b5

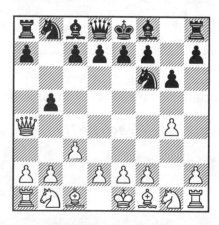

I played this game against a young fellow, at a rapid time control, in Sokolniki Park. Black's last move was aggressive. I could have taken the pawn, but refused in favor of proceeding with my general plan.

4.♕f4 ♗b7 5.♘f3 ♗g7 6.d3 d6 7.♘bd2 e5 8.♕g3 0-0 9.h4

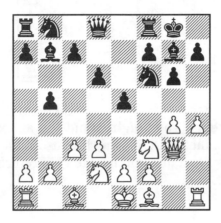

Now the general assault begins. Black keeps thinking that White is insufficiently developed and is mounting an incorrect attack. This is a kind of optimistic delusion. Why? Because my h1-rook, without making a single move, is already participating in the attack on Black's king. Also, the king's wing already has the white queen, and his pawns participate in the offensive. It is also important to understand that there is no center; that is, there is no contact in the center. Black would like to launch a counterattack in the center, but there's nothing to hook it onto.

9...h5

I consider this a mistake. In any case, not one of the classics would recommend playing a pawn this way, away from your own king.

10.♗h3 ♘bd7 11.g5 ♘d5 12.♘e4

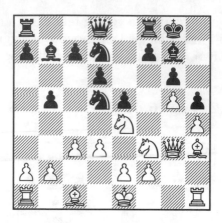

And here we see the legendary Elshad knight! It's important to understand the setup. The knight stands on an excellent square, and the f-pawn cannot drive it away because White will capture it *en passant*. Black's knight could leap to f4 in return; but we would simply chop it off.

12...♘7b6 13.♖g1

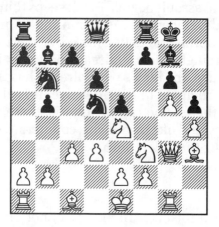

One may guess at the power behind this mysterious rook move if one visualizes White's entire attacking plan. And so: on the kingside, everything is blocked. At any rate, that's what Black is thinking.

Well, there are lots of ways to break up the position; one of these was carried out in the game. Another might go like this: White drops his knight into f6; after a couple of forced captures on that square, we open the g-file – this is what that rook on g1 is good for.

13...♗c8 14.♗g2

We're not trading pieces: first, because you don't trade off attacking pieces; and second, because the white bishop, owing to the pawn structure, is far stronger than its black counterpart.

14...♗f5

14...♖b8.

15.♘h2 ♖b8 16.♗f3 ♕e7 17.♘f1 ♖be8

17...♖bd8 18.♕h2 c6 19.♘fg3 (19.♘f6+ ♘xf6 20.gxf6 ♗xf6 21.♘g3 ♗g4 *[21...♗e6 22.♘xh5±]* 22.♗xg4 hxg4 23.h5) 19...♗e6 20.♗xh5 gxh5 21.♘xh5 ♘d7 22.♔f1 (22.a4 b4 23.c4 ♘5b6 24.a5 ♘c8 25.g6 f5 26.♗g5 ♘f6 27.♘exf6+ ♗xf6 28.♘xf6+ ♖xf6 29.h5+–; 22.♘hf6+) 22...♘c5 23.♘hf6+ ♔h8.

18.♕h2 c6 19.♘fg3

I think that it was only here that Black understood the predicament he was in.

19...♗e6 20.♗xh5

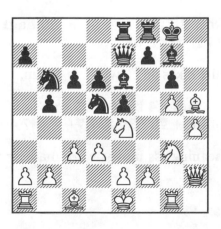

Netting two pawns for the piece, but obviously this isn't the most important factor here. The black king is totally exposed, and White has an easy time.

20...gxh5 21.♘xh5± ♘d7 22.♗d2

22.♘hf6+ ♔h8.

22...♘c5 23.♘hf6+ ♔h8 24.♘xc5 ♘xf6

24...dxc5 25.♘xe8.

25.♘xe6 fxe6 26.gxf6 ♗xf6 27.♗g5

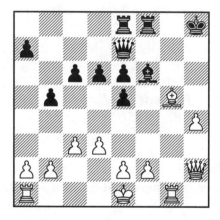

A typical transformation of the advantage: a piece is won, White remains with an extra pawn. And Black's king is still in danger.

27...d5 28.♔d2 ♖f7 29.♖g2 ♖ef8 30.♖ag1 b4 31.♗xf6+ ♕xf6 32.♖g6 ♕f5

Otherwise White takes on e5 with his queen.

33.♖1g5 ♕f4+ 34.♕xf4 bxc3+ 35.bxc3 exf4 36.♖xe6 ♖b7 37.♔c2 ♖fb8 38.♖h6+ ♖h7 39.♖xh7+ ♔xh7 40.♖f5

A few more meaningless moves were made, typical of blitz or rapid play.

1-0

54. Nemtsev_Igor (2873) – Brastam (2812)

16 October 2015

1.d3 g6 2.c3 ♗g7 3.♕a4 ♘f6

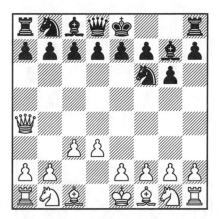

This is what fans of the King's Indian tend to play. They signal clearly that they will castle kingside, fearing nothing.

4.g4 0-0 5.g5 ♘h5

Without knowing White's ideas, this knight move would seem totally fine. The h-pawn looks completely blocked – nothing to be afraid of.

6.♗g2 d5 7.♗f3

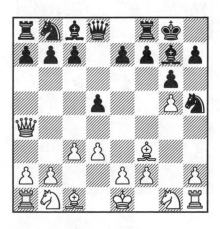

But suddenly it turns out that the knight will get whacked and Black's kingside will be left in tatters.

7...e5 8.♗xh5 gxh5 9.♕h4 ♗f5 10.♘d2 ♗g6 11.♘f1 ♘c6 12.♘g3 f6

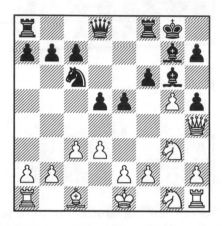

Black opens up the game, yet this was the decisive error. On the other hand, Black's position was already bad: the h5-pawn cannot be held. For me, this was all "theory;" I hadn't needed to make a single independent move.

13.♘xh5 f5 14.♘xg7± ♔xg7 15.♕g3 f4 16.♕g2 e4 17.d4! ♕e7 18.h4 f3 19.♕g3 fxe2 20.h5 ♗f5 21.g6!

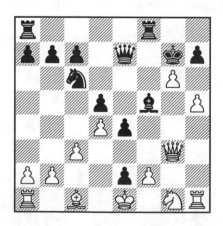

Paradoxically, Black is still unaware that White is fully into the decisive attack. Observe carefully: the bishop at c1, the rook at h1, and the queen on g3 are staring intently at Black's king, while the infantry carries out the decisive breakthrough.

21...hxg6 22.hxg6

Here I messed up: 22.♗h6+!! would have brought the game to an elegant conclusion: 22...♔xh6 (22...♔g8 23.♗xf8 ♖xf8 24.♘xe2) 23.hxg6+ ♔g7 24.♖h7+ ♔g8 25.♖xe7.

22...♖h8 23.♖h7+ ♖h7 24.gxh7+ ♔xh7 25.♘xe2 ♖g8 26.♕h2+ ♔g7 27.♗h6+ ♔f7 28.♘f4 e3 29.♕h5+ ♗g6 30. ♕xd5+ ♔e8 31.♕xg8+ ♔d7 32.♕xg6 exf2+ 33.♔xf2

White has gobbled up everything. Black's main problem was his poorly protected king.

1-0

55. Nemtsev_Igor (2848) – GabrielLanda (2664)

7 July 2015

1.d3 ♘f6 2.c3 g6 3.h3 ♗g7 4.g4

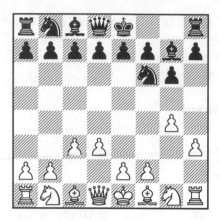

In cases like this, where Black is clearly in a hurry to develop his kingside, there is no need to disguise one's opening choices.

4...d5 5.♗g2 c5 6.♕a4+

This move brings on the craziness, thinks Black: "What a stupid check!"

6...♘c6

If 6...♗d7, then 7.♕b3 pressuring Black's queenside.

7.♘d2 0-0 8.g5 ♘h5 9.♗f3 ♘f4? 10.♘f1

Black throws away a piece, but then, in three-minute chess we frequently miss hanging pieces.

10...♖b8

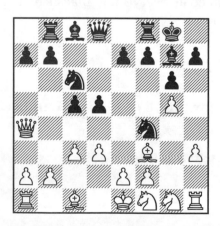

11.♕xf4

Finally I see it!

11…e5 12.♕h2 b5 13.h4 b4 14.h5 bxc3 15.hxg6 fxg6 16.♕xh7+ ♔f7 17.bxc3

17.♖h6. Of course I knew about this move; I've even played it myself a few times in similar positions. It wins instantly.

17…d4

With 17…♖h8, Black had a chance to trap the queen. On the other hand… well, check the resulting variation; I'm sure that all the chances lie with White, anyway: 18.♕xh8 ♗xh8 19.♖xh8 ♕xh8 20.♗xd5+ ♗e6 21.♗xc6⇄.

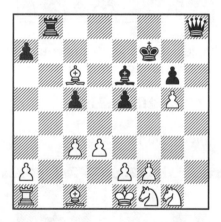

18.c4 ♗e6 19.♗xc6 ♕a5+ 20.♗d2 ♕a3 21.♖h6 ♗f5 22.♗d5+ ♔e8 23.♕xg7

Just mopping up.

23…♕b2 24.♗c6+ ♔d8 25.♕xf8+ ♔c7 26.♖h7+

26.♕e7+ ♔b6 27.♖d1 ♕c2 28.♗e4 ♔a6 29.♕xc5 ♕xa2 30.♗xf5 ♖b1 31.♖xg6+ ♔b7 32.♕e7+ ♔b8 33.♖g8#.

26…♗d7 27.♖xd7+ ♔b6 28.♕xb8+ ♔xc6 29.♕d6#

That's a mate, sir, no matter where you're from!

56. Elshad – Malyshev

1.c3 ♘f6 2.♕a4 g6 3.g4 ♗g7 4.d3 0-0 5.g5 ♘d5 6.h4 ♘b6 7.♕f4

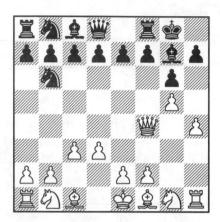

An excellent choice! Of course, White could retreat to b3 or c2, which have their own advantages and disadvantages.

7...e5 8.♕h2 d5 9.h5 ♗f5 10.♗h3

Trading off the piece that protects g6.

10...♕d7 11.hxg6 ♗xh3 12.gxf7+ ♖xf7 13.♘xh3 ♕f5 14.g6!

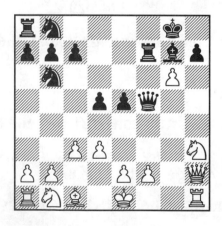

A clearance combination. The g5 square is clearly meant for a white knight.

14...hxg6 15.♘g5

Note that the knight's leap to g5 was made possible by the modest d2-d3 in the opening.

15...♖f6

Not 15...♖f8 16.♕h7#.

16.e4 dxe4 17.dxe4 ♕g4 18.♗e3 ♘c6 19.♕h7+ ♔f8 20. ♗c5+ ♖d6 21.♗xd6+ cxd6 22.♕xg6 1-0

57. nemtsevguru (2334) – jaguarxyz123 (2281)

lichess.org, 16 July 2017

1.c3 ♘f6 2.♕a4 g6 3.g4 ♗g7 4.d3 0-0 5.g5 ♘d5 6.♗g2 c6 7.h4 e5 8.h5 d6 9.♕h4 ♘f4 10.♗xf4 exf4 11.hxg6 fxg6 12. ♕xh7+ ♔f7 13.♕h2

13.♗e4 ♕xg5 (13...♗f5 14.♗xf5 gxf5 15.♘f3 ♕d7 16.♕h5+ ♔e7 17.♕g6 ♖g8 18.♘d4+−) 14.♘f3 ♕f6 15.♘h4 ♖h8 16.♕xg6+ ♕xg6 17.♗xg6+ ♔e7 18.♗e4 ♔f6 19.♘d2 d5 20.♗f3 ♗e6 21.0-0-0±.

13...♕xg5 14.♘h3 ♕f6 15.♘xf4 ♖h8 16.♕g3 ♖xh1+ 17. ♗xh1 g5 18.♘h5 ♕g6 19.♘xg7 ♔xg7 20.♘d2 ♗f5 21.♘f3 g4 22.♘h4 ♕f6 23.♘xf5+ ♕xf5 24.♗e4 ♕g5 25.♕xd6 ♘a6 26. ♕d7+ ♔f8 27.♕xb7 1-0

58. nemtsevguru (2336) – SHAFAR16 (2330)

lichess.org, 31 October 2016

1.c3 ♘f6 2.♕a4 g6 3.g4 ♗g7

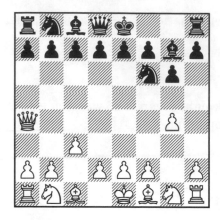

This game was played at one of the Internet portals.

4.g5

I consider it best to show one's cards right away. Now, he doesn't feel like going backwards, so – forward we go!

4...♘d5 5.♗g2 ♘b6 6.♕f4

This is what I usually play. Of course, there is also the (temporary) retreat to c2. This has its own ideas, and I'll be discussing those later on.

6...e5 7.♕g3 ♘c6 8.d3 d5 9.h4

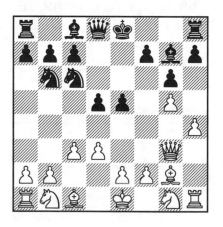

Black sees that castling kingside would be dangerous, and so he brings out his queenside pieces rapidly in order to castle there.

9...♗e6 10.h5 ♛d6 11.♘d2

There is no need to rush the h-pawn capture. In such structures (the Yugoslav Attack, for example), for Black to capture on h5 will as a rule be unfavorable. Meanwhile, the h5-pawn worries Black a lot. Where is it going? And when? He always has to be calculating its possible movements. And meanwhile, his clock is running, tick-tock, tick-tock...

11...0-0-0 12.a4

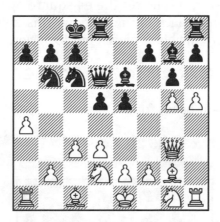

Now that the king has gone away to the queen's wing, I open a second front there. The a4-a5 battering ram looks (and is) very dangerous, so Black's reaction is understandable.

12...a5 13.♛h4

Preparing my queen to reverse course from the kingside to the queenside.

13...d4

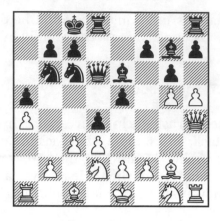

What can one say here? "I've got to do something," Black thinks. So he does what he was taught to do: to attempt a breakthrough in the center. However, this leaves the e4 square open to the Elshad knight. Here's what Black did not know: this knight is arguably stronger than all of the black pieces put together.

14.♘e4! ♛e7 15.h6 ♝f8 16.♘f3 ♛d7 17.♘f6 ♛d6 18.♘d2

One more knight heads for e4.

18...dxc3 19.bxc3 ♝d5 20.♘de4

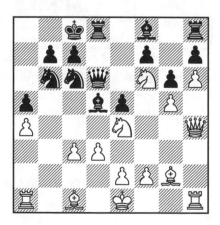

White has a number of ways to win, 20.♝a3 for example.

20...♗xe4 21.♗xe4 ♗e7 22.♗a3 ♕e6 23.♗g2 ♗xf6 24.♗h3

The queen is skewered; Black resigned.

1-0

59. Nemtsev_Igor (2802) – allecsander (2670)

28 May 2017

1.c3 ♘f6 2.♕a4 g6 3.g4 ♗g7 4.♗g2

This is White's most accurate continuation. Why? The point is that we are planning to hit at the f6-knight with the pawn on g5. If our bishop is already on g2, then the knight can either go back to e8 or move to h5. If it goes to h5, we'll fire on it with ♗f3, breaking up the black kingside pawns.

4...0-0 5.g5 ♘e8 6.h4

It's equally necessary to get the h-pawn's advance in as quickly as possible, so that our queen can move to h4 in timely fashion.

6...c5

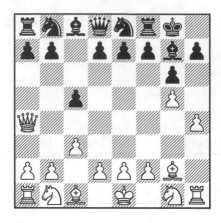

7.h5 ♘c7 8.♕h4 ♖e8

Another *tabiya* in the Elshad. There's no direct mate (yet), but White does have a strong attack, plus a psychological advantage: we know what to do and therefore play quickly and confidently, while our opponent is laboriously looking for a way to defend.

9.hxg6 hxg6 10.d3 d5 11.♗f4 e5 12.♗e3 d4 13.♗d2 ♘c6 14.♘f3

No use at all, on any of the preceding moves, giving check on h7 — because Black, according to the rules of chess, would have only one reply, ...♔f8. Better to let Black puzzle over when we're going to play that check at h7.

14...♗f5 15.♗h3!

Taking away one of the king's defenders.

15...♗xh3 16.♖xh3 ♛d7 17.♘h2

A fairly typical means of getting at Black's king.

17...♘d5 18.♘g4 ♛f5

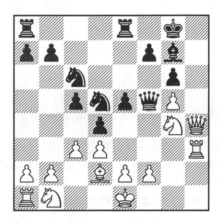

There is no longer any good defense.

19.♘h6+ ♗xh6 20.♛xh6 ♛xh3

Otherwise it's mate right away. The remaining game moves are given only because, it being a three-minute game, Black didn't want to resign. Black's feeling of irritation was enormous; and, through inertia, he played on until mate.

This makes a lot more sense over the Internet than it would in an over-the-board game. Your opponent might have to leave the site, or the Internet might freeze up on him. It does happen sometimes.

21.♛xh3 e4 22.dxe4 ♖xe4 23.♛d7 dxc3 24.♛xd5 cxb2 25.♗c3 bxa1♛ 26.♗xa1 ♖ae8 27.e3 ♘d4 28.♘d2 ♖4e5 29. ♛c4 b5 30.♛c3 b4 31.♛c4 ♘f5 32.♗xe5 ♖xe5 33.♛a6 ♔g7 34.♛xa7 ♘xe3 35.fxe3 ♖xe3+ 36.♔d1 ♖a3 37.♛xc5 ♖xa2 38.♛xb4 ♖xd2+ 39.♔xd2 ♔g8 40.♛d4 1-0

60. Papin – Golikov

1.c3 g6 2.♕a4 ♗g7 3.g4 ♘c6 4.♗g2 ♘f6 5.h4

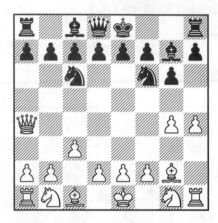

A good way to conduct the attack. Its relative shortcoming is that right now there are too many pawns sitting on the fourth rank, and they interfere with the white queen's moving to h4. On the other hand, pretty soon everything reverts to its proper place.

5...0-0 6.g5 ♘e8

6...♘h5 7.♗f3, followed by taking on h5.

7.h5 b5 8.♕h4 f5

You meet this error fairly frequently. No one notices the bishop on g2: it's a sort of optical illusion. From g2, the bishop scans the queen's wing, while it can also swiftly join in the attack against the king.

9.d3 ♖b8 10.♗d5+ e6 11.♗xc6 dxc6 12.hxg6 hxg6 13. ♕h7+ ♔f7 14.♖h6

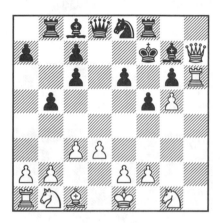

And that's it: the g6 square cannot be defended. A standard attack, of which there are many in this book.

1-0

61. Elshad – Aliev

1.c3 ♘f6 2.♕a4 g6 3.g4

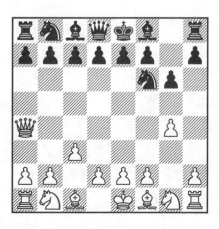

Still another fianchetto-crush.

3...♗g7 4.♗g2 c5 5.d3 0-0 6.g5 ♘e8 7.h4 ♘c6 8.h5 ♕a5

A naive attempt to trade queens. The problem is that Black doesn't understand the point of the opening. In fact, he can't conceive where the white queen intends to go.

9.♕h4

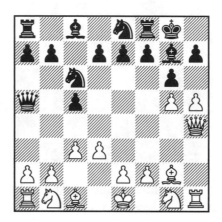

9...♘d4 10.hxg6

In this position, of course, no player of White is interested in the a1-rook.

10...fxg6 11.♘f3 ♘c2+ 12.♔d1 ♘xa1

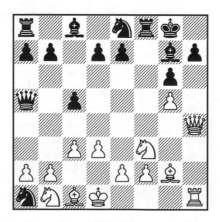

13.♕xh7+ ♔f7 14.♘e5+

Or 14.♖h6 ♔e6 15.♕xg6+ ♗f6 16.♗h3+.

The most brutal way was 13.♘e5 d6 14.♕xh7#.

14...♔e6 15.♕xg6+ ♗f6 16.♗h3+ ♔xe5 17.♗f4+ 1-0

62. Elshad – Krasnov

8 September 1999

1.c3 g6 2.♕a4 ♗g7 3.d3 ♘f6 4.g4

It makes sense to play this way, without h2-h3, since Black has already shown clearly where he intends to castle.

4...e5 5.♗g2 0-0 6.g5 ♘h5

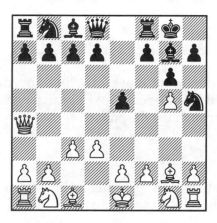

Time after time, new "refuters" of the Elshad Opening walk right into our well-known snares.

7.♗f3

Black didn't see this move before, because a sort of optical illusion was in place, where he thought that the only reason the bishop came out to g2 was to attack his queenside.

7...f5 8.gxf6 *e.p.*

This is better than capturing on h5. Generally speaking, in such positions it's better to take *en passant* in order to open up lines on the kingside. Curiously, Black often thinks, in these circumstances, that he's the one attacking on the kingside.

8...♘f6 9.h4 d5 10.♗g5 ♕d6 11.♘d2 ♘c6 12.♗xf6 ♗xf6 13.♕b3

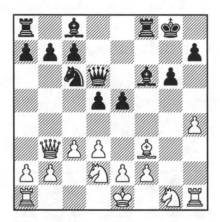

Another very important move in White's overall construction. The queen goes to b3, where it looks at the pawn on b7 as well as at Black's king through the d5-pawn.

13...♗e6 14.♘h3

White can capture on b7, so long as Black's rook cannot get to b8 in order to retaliate by swooping down to b2.

14...♗xh4 15.0-0-0 b5 16.♖dg1 e4 17.♗g4 exd3 18.exd3 ♗xf2 19.♘g5 ♗xg4 20.♖xg4 ♗e3 21.♖g2 ♘e5 22.♘xh7 ♘xd3+ 23.♔b1 ♘f4 24.♘xf8 ♘xg2 25.♘e4

The reader is advised to work out for him- or herself all the most beautiful variations in this game.

25...♕e5 26.♘f6+ ♔f7

26...♕xf6 27.♕xd5+.

27.♖h7+ ♔xf6 28.♘d7+

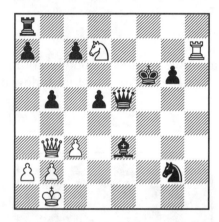

A most elegant finish. There's no point in flooding the analysis with computer variations. Set it up on the board, and work them out for yourself. That will be much more useful to you.

1-0

63. Elshad – Voropayev

2000

1.c3 ♘f6 2.♕a4 ♘c6 3.g4 g6 4.♗g2 ♗g7 5.d3 0-0 6.g5

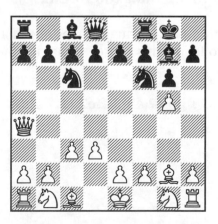

Generally, chess thinking says that the pawns should be in front of the pieces, as in battle, when the foot soldiers are in front of the officers. But here Black's knights clearly are out of place, in front of their pawns. Why shouldn't White annoy them a little?

6...♘h5

A most natural move. Indeed, nobody could have predicted White's next move, or the maneuvers that follow it.

7.♗f3

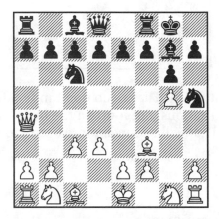

Whoa – it turns out that the black knight has no place to go: the f4 square is guarded by the white queen.

7...d6 8.♕h4 e5 9.♗xh5 gxh5 10.♘d2

This is better than recapturing with the queen. In any event, the knight is going to follow this route, so that it's the knight netting the h5-pawn.

10...♗f5 11.♘f1 ♗g6 12.♘g3 ♘e7 13.♘xh5

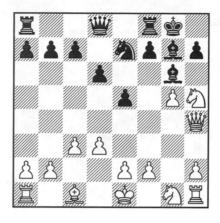

Evaluate White's idea. From h5, the knight wants to land on f6. White's rook intends to move to g1. And the queen's bishop (from its starting square, c1) is already eyeing the dark squares around the black king.

13...♘f5 14.♕h3 ♖e8 15.e4 ♘e7 16.♘f6+ ♗xf6 17.gxf6 ♘c6 18.♗g5 h5 19.f3 a5 20.♘e2 b5 21.♘g3 b4 22.♘xh5

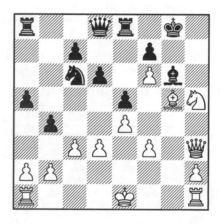

And that is basically it. There is no defense against the invasion of White's queen via the h-file.

1-0

64. Elshad – Nasirov

2000

1.c3 ♘f6 2.♕a4 g6 3.g4 b5

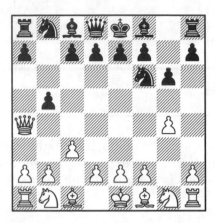

Original and interesting. Black does not intend to swim with the current, but makes his own splash!

4.♕xb5 ♘xg4 5.♗g2 c6 6.♕a4 h5 7.h3 ♘f6 8.d3

Beginning the unfolding of forces normal for this opening.

8...♕b6 9.♘f3 a5 10.♘bd2 ♘a6 11.♕h4

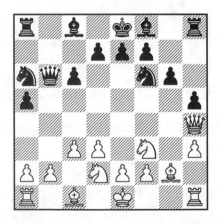

The exact moment for White to redeploy his queen. The g-file is opened for White's rook, while there is no danger to White from Black's forces.

11...♘c5 12.♘c4 ♕d8 13.♗e3 ♘a4 14.♘ce5

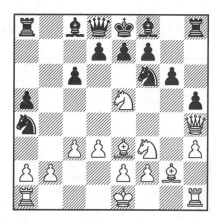

Unexpected. Effective. Powerful. From the looks of things, why shouldn't the pawn on b2 be taken?

14...♘xb2 15.♘g5

Although this kind of move isn't all that hard to find – still, it's easy to miss!

15...♖g8 16.♘gxf7 ♕c7 17.♗c1 ♖b8 18.♗f4 d6

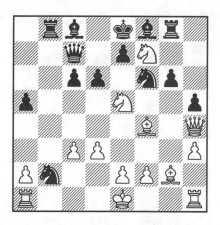

It looks like the white knight must die. Well, if he dies – let there be music with it!

19.♘xd6+ ♕xd6 20.♘c4 ♘xd3+ 21.exd3 ♕e6+ 22.♔f1 ♖a8 23.♖e1 ♕d7 24.♕xf6 ♕xd3+ 25.♔g1 ♕xc4 26.♕xc6+

At the end of the combination, a cold shower. Black is simply a rook down.

26...♕xc6 27.♗xc6+ ♔f7 28.♗d5+ e6 29.♗xa8

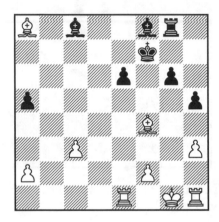

1-0

65. Elshad – Salnykov

2000

1.c3 ♘f6 2.♕a4 g6 3.g4 ♗g7 4.♗g2 c6 5.d3 d5 6.g5

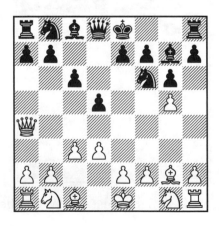

White deliberately waited for Black to play ...d7-d5 before playing g4-g5. Why? To give Black the chance to play ...♘f6-d7, further away from his king.

6...♘fd7 7.h4 ♘b6 8.♕b4

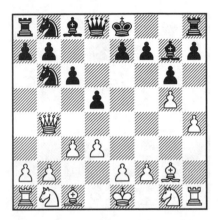

As though foreseeing the original play that follows, White's queen stays on the fourth rank.

8...♘8d7 9.h5 ♘f8

Clearly, Black considers castling to be a risky move here.

10.h6

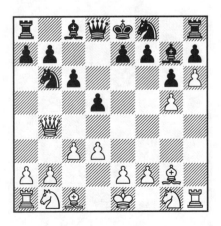

This is unexpected. Why? Because the bishop does have a retreat square. And White's kingside play appears to have come to an end?!

10...♗e5 11.♘f3 ♗d6 12.♕d4 ♖g8

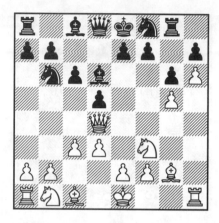

It's unreasonable to expect that Black could have predicted White's next move...

13.♕g7

Black's rook is trapped!

13...♖xg7 14.hxg7 e5 15.g8♕

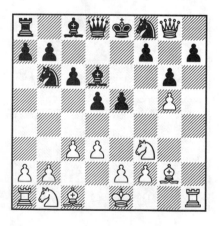

Beautiful! I never tire of praising Elshad's games to the heavens!!

1-0

66. Amannazarov – Nizhegorodtsev

1.c3 ♞f6 2.♕a4 g6 3.g4

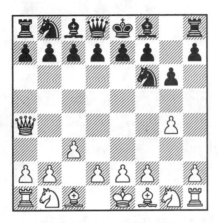

This is the right move in this type of position. If the g-pawn goes on the attack at once, then the h-pawn may also go immediately to h4, instead of implementing slower "standard" ideas like h2-h3.

3...♝g7 4.♝g2 ♞c6 5.d3 d5

Generally speaking, this development with the knight on c6 and a pawn on d5 is inferior to the panzer setup with pawns on c6 and d5. Why? The problem is White's bishop at g2: it now has more chances to flex its muscles up the long diagonal.

6.g5 ♞h5

As we have seen, this is a typical reaction in the Yugoslav Attack, where the move is played so as to block the white h-pawn's advance to h5.

7.♗f3

This is a weapon we see quite often in this book. And it's no accident! When our opponent sees this, only then does he come to understand that his kingside is about to get wrecked. The plan would have been even better had Black castled already. We have seen other games like this earlier on.

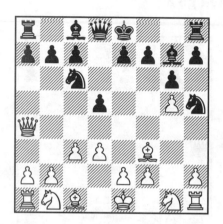

7...0-0 8.♘d2 e5 9.♗xh5 gxh5 10.♘f1

10.♕h4 was better.

10...d4

Now that queen move is impossible.

11.♕c2 b5 12.♘f3 ♗b7 13.♘g3

Imagine if the white queen were already on h4.

13...h4 14.♘xh4 ♘e7 15.♖g1

We will not forget about the rook.

15...♕d7 16.♘e4

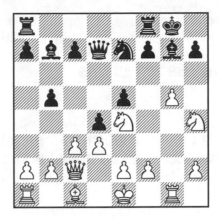

White has another possibility here – namely, 16.cxd4, with the further idea of bringing the queen to c5 and then to h5: 16...exd4 17.♘h5 ♘g6 18.♘f6+ ♗xf6 19.gxf6 ♖fe8 (it might seem as though it's Black attacking the white king, via e2) 20.♕c5 ♕e6 21.♕h5 (as it turns out, the white queen was not only defending, but at the same time also attacking the black king) 21...♕xf6 22.♗g5 ♕e5 23.f4 ♕e3 24.♖g3 ♕e6 25.f5 ♕e5 26.fxg6 fxg6 27.♘xg6 ♕xe2+ (else White mates) 28.♕xe2 ♖xe2+ 29.♔xe2 hxg6+–. The smoke clears and White is a rook up.

16...♗xe4 17.dxe4 ♖ad8 18.♘f5 ♘xf5 19.exf5 e4 20.f6

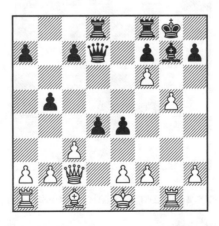

A curious position. In effect, Black is playing a piece down, but it seems to him that he is attacking the white king, which is "stranded"

in the center. The problem for our opponents is that they don't understand that, in principle, we don't aim to castle in the Elshad.

20...d3 21.♕d1 ♗h8 22.♖g3 ♕d5

22...♖fe8 23.b4.

23.♗e3 ♖fe8 24.b4 ♕c4 25.♕b3 a6 26.♖d1 ♖d5 27.♗d4 dxe2 28.♖d2 e3 29.♗xe3 ♕xb3 30.axb3 ♖xd2 31.♔xd2 h6 32.h4 ♔h7 33.♔xe2 ♔g6

The black king has escaped from its prison – but what about the bishop?

34.♔d3 ♖d8+ 35.♔e4 ♔h5 36.gxh6

A concrete solution to the position – and an absolutely correct one!

36...♗xf6 37.♗g5 ♗xg5 38.hxg5 ♔g6 39.f4 f5+ 40.gxf6+ ♔xf6 41.h7 ♖e8+ 42.♔d5 ♖h8 43.♖h3

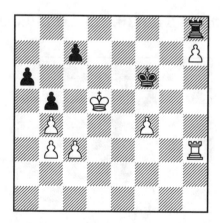

Two extra pawns guarantee White an easy win.

1-0

//

Black Plays ...♘f6 and ...e7-e6

67. Elshad – Grigoriants

1.c3 ♘f6 2.♕a4 e6 3.g4 ♗e7 4.♗g2 0-0

Playing Black against Elshad is the Moscow grandmaster, Sergei Grigoriants. He has selected an unpretentious system of development, probably intending to outplay his lower-rated opponent later on. In that sense, the Elshad Opening is just exactly the system of play that one can and should employ against stronger opponents.

Why? Think about it: if we adopt a theoretical opening or variation in a game against a GM, he is bound to know it better than we do; and it will be precisely the stronger player who tempts us onto unfamiliar territory. So let him find his way in a position of our choosing from the very start.

5.g5 ♘d5

Most players of Black here move away their knight exactly like this. But there are games in this book where the knight goes back to e8 instead.

6.h4 ♞b6 7.♛c2

Besides the text move, it's also possible to move the queen to the kingside right away – say, with ♛a4-f4-h2 or ♛a4-f4-g3.

7...c5 8.d3 d5 9.♞d2 ♞c6 10.♞f1

10.♔f1 e5.

So far, nothing new. White carries out the standard piece maneuvers for this opening, preparing to attack Black's king. Meanwhile Black thinks, at least, that all this is disrespect for chess, or perhaps something like a personal insult. And that is precisely what we need: to take our opponent out of his comfort zone. Let him feel nervous.

10...e5 11.♞g3 f5

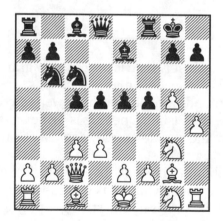

No doubt Black thinks he's launching a decisive attack on White's king. In a position like this, we have to capture *en passant* – remember this!

12.gxf6 *e.p.* ♝xf6 13.♞f3 ♝g4 14.a4

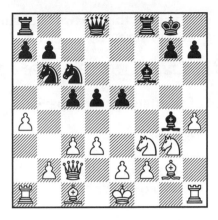

No doubt Black thought that he was starting a decisive attack on White's king. In this position, you just have to take *en passant*. Remember this moment.

One more strategic juncture in this game. The a-pawn is supposed to drive the black knight away from b6 – but why? Two objectives: the first is that, obviously, the knight will be driven to an inferior post, weakening the d5-pawn. And the second – we'll talk about that one later.

14...c4 15.dxc4 ♞xc4 16.♞g5

Threatens mate on the move.

16...g6 17.b3 ♞b6 18.a5 ♞c8 19.a6 bxa6

A double-edged decision.

20.♖a4

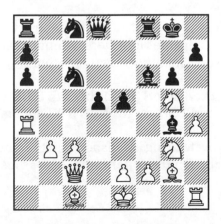

Here is the second point of the a-pawn battering ram: the rook enters the fight via the fourth rank.

20...e4 21.f3 ♗e5 22.♘f1 ♕f6 23.♗d2 ♘b6 24.♘e3 ♗h5

Probably afraid of an attack by the h-pawn.

25.♖xa6 ♖ac8 26.♖xb6!

The d5 square (and, eventually, all the important squares on the board) will soon be occupied by White's pieces.

26...axb6 27.♘xd5 ♕d6 28.♕xe4

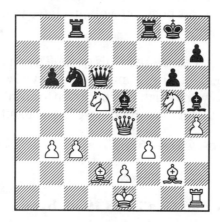

Look at this position. Indeed, whose king is in greater danger here?

28...♖fe8 29.♕c4 ♔g7 30.♘e4 ♕e6 31.♗h3 ♘a5 32.♕d3

You've got to hand it to White's fighting spirit. Certainly he could have gone for the endgame right here, winning back the exchange and coming out with a material advantage, plus the better position.

32...♕c6 33.♗xc8 ♕xc8 34.♘xb6 ♕f5 35.b4 ♘b3 36.♕d7+ ♕xd7 37.♘xd7 ♘xd2 38.♔xd2 ♖d8 39.♘ec5 g5

While attempting to bring his bishop into the game, Black makes a decisive oversight. On the other hand, he was lost anyway.

40.♘e6+ 1-0

68. Elshad – Konstantin Lobach

20 May 2015

1.c3 ♘f6 2.♕a4 e6

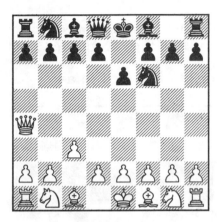

A typical reaction to an unusual opening. Konstantin Lobach, a real fighter, fearless and redoubtable! In Sokolniki Park he has a reputation as a strong player, and he is known for a correct approach to interpersonal relations.

3.g4 ♗e7 4.♗g2 0-0 5.g5 ♘d5 6.h4 f6

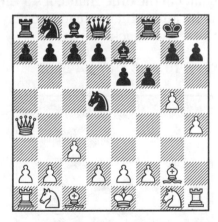

Quite often, those who face the Elshad think that they are attacking the king. At this point, it looks like Black is opening the f-file for this reason.

7.gxf6 ♗xf6 8.d3 ♘b6 9.♕c2 ♗xh4?

A mistake. But doesn't it feel like Black is the one attacking?

10.♘f3 ♗f6 11.♘bd2

The standard decision, but there was also another interesting attacking possibility: 11.d4!? g6 12.♗h6 ♖e8 13.e4→.

11...d5 12.♘f1 e5 13.♘g3 ♗g4 14.a4

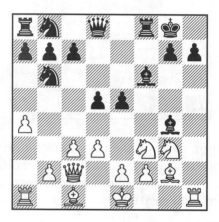

Elshad often does this to change the course of the game and confuse his opponent. On the other hand, it's a very sound idea to chase away the knight, after which he can also play ♖a1-a4, adding this soldier to the attack on Black's king.

14...a5 15.♕b3 c5 16.♗e3 ♕c7 17.♘g5!

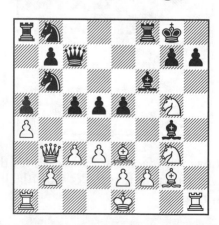

As it turns out, the Achilles' heel of this position is the pawn on d5.

17...♗xg5 18.♗xd5+ ♘xd5 19.♕xd5+ ♕f7 20.♕xf7+ ♖xf7 21.♗xg5 ♘c6 22.♘e4

Here Black ran out of time, but White has the upper hand. Play might continue 22...b6 23.f3 ♗f5 24.♘d6 ♖ff8 25.0-0-0 ♗g6 26.♘c4±, and White's pawns start rolling. Also, take a look at the white pawn chain: Black can't get near it.

1-0

69. Nemtsev_Igor (2685) – Dmitri_Batsanin (2871)

20 February 2015

1.c3 e6 2.♕a4 ♘f6 3.g4 ♗e7 4.g5 ♘d5 5.h4 ♘c6 6.♗g2 ♘b6 7.♕g4

My opponent, an international master, is a constant visitor to the "Chess Planet" portal. We have played each other many times, mostly in tournaments, with a roughly even score. In this game, there was a lot that was instructive, and even humorous. You will witness the cross-transfer of entire populations of chess pieces, from one wing to the other and then back again.

7...d5 8.d3 e5 9.♕g3 ♗e6 10.♘d2 ♗d6 11.h5

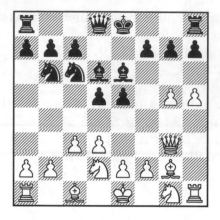

Even such a hardened fighter as Dmitri would be terrified of castling kingside here, and so he starts preparing to castle long.

11...♕e7 12.♕h4

But now I, too, prepare to swing my queen back to the queenside from the opposite wing.

12...0-0-0

This looks very good. All of Black's pieces are now developed, and quite well, at that. What White can do is not very clear yet to us... nor is it to his opponent!

13.a4

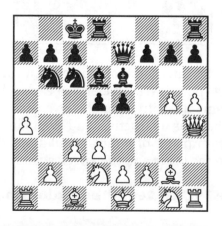

This is White's basic concept in the Elshad. As the white king stays in the center, the rooks consequently remain in their places. Like guns, they fire over their own pawns. That is, the rooks' activity begins right on their starting squares, so they don't even need to develop the standard way.

13...f5 14.a5 ♘d7 15.a6 b6 16.♕a4

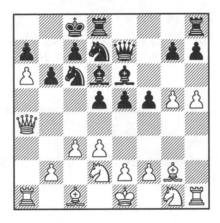

The queen has redeployed once again, and like a wintry wind, the long diagonal is "whistling." My opponent starts evacuating his king once again, now back to the kingside. This is the most amusing game in the entire book!

16...♘cb8 17.c4 ♘c5 18.♕a2 dxc4 19.♗b7+ ♔d7 20.♘xc4 ♔e8

At this point, my opponent had very little time left. And why? Simple: up to here, I had hardly made any independent moves. All of my moves so far had been either previously approved by me or analyzed at home.

21.b4 ♘cd7 22.♗d2 ♔f8 23.♕b2 ♗f7 24.h6

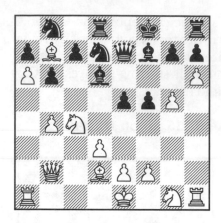

How do you like that? Now the h-pawn is preparing much the same opening of a long-diagonal as did the a-pawn on the queenside.

24...gxh6 25.♖xh6 ♗g6 26.♘f3 ♖g8 27.♗d5 ♖g7 28.♘xd6 ♕xd6 29.♗c4 e4

Apparently tired of defending threats, real and imagined, my opponent decided that it was time to deliver a blow in the center, without taking into account the fact that the long diagonal has come open. Now it's all over.

30.♘d4 ♘c6 31.♘e6+

Forcing Black to give up his queen, as otherwise my queen takes the g7-rook, with mate.

31...♕xe6 32.♗xe6 ♖e7

Why continue the game, you ask? The answer is that it's a three-minute game, and anything can happen.

33.♗xd7 *[33.♕h8# – Tr.]* **♖exd7 34.♕h8+ ♔e7 35.♕f6+ ♔e8 36.♖xg6**

Competent and professional *[except for move 33! – Tr.]*. When you're a queen ahead, you just need to trade everything off as quickly as possible.

36...hxg6 37.♕xg6+ ♔e7 38.♕xc6 exd3 39.♕f6+ ♔e8 40.exd3 ♖xd3 41.♗e3 ♖8d6 42.♕xf5 ♔e7 43.♖c1 ♔d8 44. ♔e2 ♖3d5 45.♕f7 ♖d7 46.♕f8#

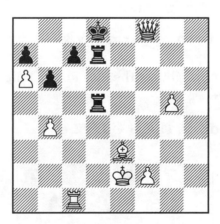

70. Nemtsev_Igor (2833) – Timoshenko_Aleksandr (2194)

25 February 2015

1.c3 e6 2.♕a4 ♘f6 3.g4 c6 4.g5 b5

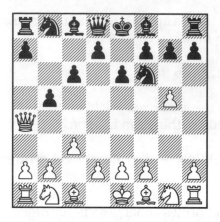

The position is certainly original, to the greatest degree possible. Here is where I play in different ways: sometimes my queen goes to h4, sometimes to f4 – sometimes even to b3.

5.♕c2 ♘d5 6.d3

Let's not neglect the g5-pawn.

6...♗e7 7.h4 ♗b7 8.♗g2 c5 9.♘f3

Otherwise Black might get the idea for the knight to jump from d5 to, let's say, b4.

9...a6 10.♘bd2 d6 11.♘f1 ♘d7 12.e4

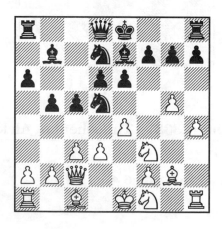

In fact, White still had some useful moves before starting to force matters. For example, he had 12.♘g3, intending ♘h5. Nevertheless, I considered it a possibility to show some initiative, since Black would hardly be castling queenside and leaving his king on e8 wouldn't be healthy, as that would interfere with the coordination of his pieces on the eighth rank. All in all, under the flag of "must moves" comes the need to hide the king away somewhere.

12...♘c7 13.♘g3 ♖c8 14.a4

However, since the king hasn't castled yet, one may irritate him on the queenside. The threat is a4xb5, followed by ♖a1-a7.

14...b4 15.♗e3 d5 16.♗f4 c4 17.d4 dxe4 18.♘xe4 ♘d5 19.♗d2 bxc3 20.bxc3 0-0

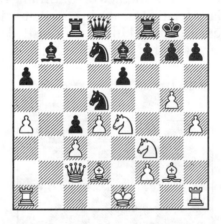

Black can hold out no longer and finally castles kingside. In any event, this was necessary, since the normal moves in this position were at an end.

21.h5

Of course, we go on the attack immediately!

21...♕a5 22.♖g1

The rook goes into ambush. If the occasion arises, I can play ♘f6(+).

22...♖fe8 23.g6

Here I decided to use this method of continuing the attack, which is typical for Sicilian variations featuring opposite-side castling. The only difference here is that my king has not castled queenside. That is, Black lacks a target for his counterattack.

23...fxg6 24.hxg6 h6 25.♗h3

One of White's important ideas. For my opponent, this is all very stressful. He believes that he has played "correctly;" and yet his position keeps getting worse and worse. Meanwhile, there's the tick-tock, tick-tock...

25...♖c6 26.♘eg5

Even if this sacrifice were not 100% correct, reacting to it is very difficult in the context of a three-minute game. I can give you this advice: if someone offers you a sacrifice, accept it at once. Will you get mated? Maybe. But using up some seconds in calculation isn't a realistic option. Take the piece – he might not find the mate.

26...♗xg5 27.♘xg5 ♘7f6

Black feared the opening of the h-file.

28.♘f7 ♘h5 29.♘e5 ♘hf4 30.♗f1 ♕c7 31.♖g4 ♘h5 32.♖b1 ♘hf6 33.♖h4 ♘d7 34.♘xc6 ♗xc6

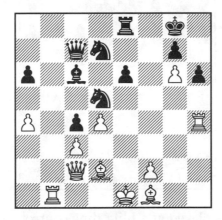

This was pretty easy for me to play: I've played positions like this many times and know the typical moves.

35.♗xh6

This shot cries out to be made.

35...♘5f6 36.♗xg7

Forcing him to take the bishop anyway.

36...♔xg7 37.♕d2 ♖h8 38.♖xh8 ♔xh8 39.♕h6+ ♔g8 40. ♗h3 ♗d5 41.g7

My opponent ran out of time. White has a won position: ♕h8 is the threat.

1-0

71. Nemtsev – NN

28 November 2015

1.d3 ♘f6 2.c3 e6 3.♕a4 ♗e7 4.g4

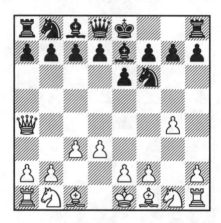

This game was played at a blitz time control, at the chess club in Sokolniki Park, Moscow. Unfortunately, there's no way to find out what my opponent's name was.

4...0-0

Black simply castles, since in fact it just was not possible to see how White was going to conduct his kingside attack.

5.♗g2 h6

This is a mistake, of course. The threat of g4-g5 proves to be less dangerous than this target for White's attack. Preferable is 5...d5.

6.h4 d5 7.g5

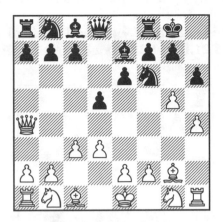

7...♘h5

7...hxg5? would be tantamount to consenting to checkmate: 8.hxg5 ♘e8 9.♕h4 f6 10.♕h7+ ♔f7 11.g6#.

8.♗f3

Oops! Here's the move that is typically unexpected to Black but familiar to Elshad practitioners.

8...g6 9.♗xh5 gxh5 10.gxh6 ♔h7 11.♘f3 ♗f6 12.♕f4 c5 13.♘bd2 ♘c6 14.♘f1 e5 15.♕e3

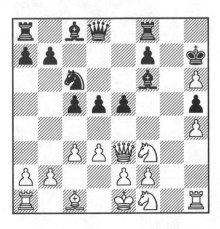

Deliberate provocation. I needed to occupy e4 with my pieces – but how? This is why I put my queen where it could get attacked.

15...d4 16.♕e4+ ♚h8 17.♘g3 ♗g4 18.♘g5 ♗xg5 19.hxg5 f5 20.gxf6 ♕xf6 21.f3 h4 22.♕xg4 hxg3 23.♕g7+

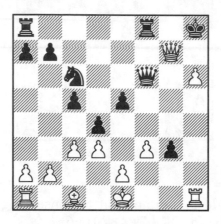

The simplest. During play, especially in the course of an attack on the king, you must remember that it's not always necessary to attack with your last ounce of strength, eyes bulging, especially if you can get a technically winning endgame.

23...♕xg7 24.hxg7+ ♚xg7 25.♗h6+ ♚f6 26.♗xf8 ♖xf8

27.♖h7 ♘e7 28.♚f1 ♘f5 29.♚g2 ♖g8 30.♖g1 ♚g6

30...♞e3+ 31.♔h3.

31.♖xb7 ♔g5 32.♖h1 1-0

Black's clock ran out, but his position was hopeless in any case.

72. ivanNikonov (1293) – rhayes12 (1291)

Live Chess Chess.com, 1 August 2017

1.c3

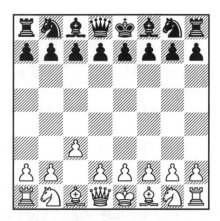

This game was sent to me by a fan of the Elshad Opening. He conducted the attack wonderfully.

1...e6 2.♕a4 ♞e7

This you definitely would not label a "refutation" of the Elshad.

3.g4 h6 4.♗g2 g6 5.h3 ♗g7 6.d3 0-0

Of course, the two players' ratings aren't very high. Thus it's quite conceivable that Black would find it a possibility to castle short.

7.♞d2 d5 8.♞f1 ♗d7 9.♕c2 c5 10.♞g3 b5 11.h4 a5 12.h5

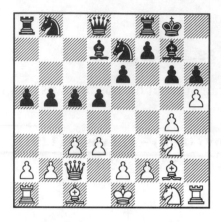

Brilliant! Here is a new attacking idea. Black's reply looks perfectly normal.

12...g5 13.f4 a4

Black plays as though nothing were happening on the kingside.

14.fxg5 hxg5 15.♗xg5 b4 16.h6

The start of the direct attack.

16...♗h8 17.h7+ ♔g7 18.♘h5+ ♔g6 19.d4+

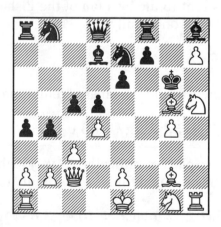

This is the sort of position where it's apparent to the naked eye that the black king is about to get mated.

19...♚xg5 20.♘h3+ ♚xg4 21.♗f3+ ♚h4 22.♛d2 e5 23. ♛g5#

And yet it was not so long ago that Black's king thought that it was safely tucked away behind its defenders.

Chapter 5

///

Black Plays ...f7-f5, Dutch Defense Style

73. Elshad – Izotov

1.c3 e6 2.♕a4 f5

When we deploy the Elshad Opening, we will sometimes encounter players who use "their" opening and nothing else. In this case, it's the Dutch Defense. If only Elshad's opponent had known that White's plan included g2-g4...

3.g4 fxg4

The most natural capture. Black thinks that the queen will now recapture on g4 and his knight will develop with tempo.

3...♘f6 is a reasonable alternative. White has two sensible choices here:

1) 4.g5, exerting pressure on the kingside. After 4...♘d5, 5.d3 leaves the fourth rank open for the white queen to shuttle over to the kingside. Following 5...♘b6, 6.♕h4 creates intolerable discomfort for the black king. After all, in the Dutch it's usually Black who figures to be attacking on the kingside.

2) 4.gxf5, which is also completely in the spirit of the opening. This opens the g-file for White's rook and the a2-g8 diagonal for White's queen. After this move, Black can play 4...exf5 5.d3 ♘c6 6.♗g2 d5 7.♘h3 ♗e7 8.♗g5 0-0 9.♘f4 (Black has played the most

natural moves, yet he stands badly) 9...♔h8 10.h4, with a powerful attack. Among other threats, White can push the pawn to h5, and somewhere along the line White's knight will leap to g6. White can also just play 10.♗xf6 ♗xf6 11.♘xd5, winning a pawn.

If you play this position in blitz or rapid chess, you will have already won a full minute (at least) by this time.

4.d3

Or 4.h3. This is one of the basic moves in this opening. If Black greedily accepts this pawn (and why shouldn't he?!?), White will enjoy an enormous initiative: 4...gxh3 (4...g3!? is probably a better try, e.g. 5.fxg3 ♘f6 6.g4 ♗e7 7.d3 0-0 8.♘f3, with mutual chances) 5.♘xh3 ♘f6 6.♘g5 (it looks like White is angling for the h7-pawn) 6...h6 7.♘xe6 (nope!) 7...b5 8.♕xb5 c6 9.♕xb8 ♖xb8 10.♘xd8 ♔xd8 11.d3±.

4...♘c6 5.♘d2 b6 6.♗g2 ♗b7

7.h3

Necessary but strong. White is always sacrificing a pawn in the Elshad. Of course, the engines say that taking it is not necessary, but this is not so obvious to Black – and besides, why shouldn't he take the pawn?

7...gxh3 8.♞xh3 ♞f6

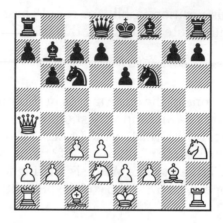

9.♕h4

White's main idea has now come to pass. But here there is another idea, no less powerful: 9.♞f4!? ♝e7 10.♞xe6 (will you agree that you hadn't seen this move before?) 10...dxe6 11.♝xc6+ ♝xc6 12.♕xc6+ ♚f8 13.♜g1±. Typical Black ruination. And no feelings of sadness on White's part.

9...♝e7

Just trying to finish development.

9...g6 (watch what happens when Black tries to fianchetto) 10.♞f1 ♝g7 11.♝h6 0-0 12.♝xg7 ♚xg7 13.♞g5. You will see this kind of attack quite often. Characteristically, the white rook joins in without making a move. 13...♞h5 (13...h5 is an attempt to close off the h-file: 14.♜g1 – OK, we're not too proud; we'll just switch over to the g-file) 14.♞g3 ♞xg3. An accommodating move, allowing us to show off the following little mate! 15.♕xh7+ ♚f6 16.fxg3 ♚xg5 17.♕h4+ ♚f5 18.♕f4#:

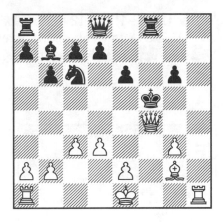

10.♘g5 ♘a5

10...h6. Our opponents always seem to want to play this move. They imagine they're attacking my knight, but things are not what they seem due to White's pin against the rook: 11.♘de4 0-0 12.♕g3 hxg5 13.♘xg5 ♘a5 14.♕h2+−. Check it out for yourself: there is no longer any realistic defense.

11.e4

Natural and strong. White simply wants to shove the black knight aside with this pawn.

11.♗xb7!? (this position is so rich in ideas that I would like to demonstrate a couple more) 11...♘xb7 12.♕g3 0-0 13.♘c4 ♘c5 14.♕h3 (a direct threat against the h7-pawn) 14...h6 15.d4 hxg5 (what else?) 16.♘e5 g4 17.♕h8#:

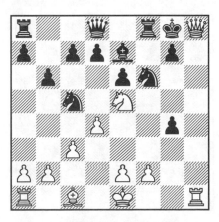

And then there's this: 11.♘de4!? h6 12.♘xf6+ ♗xf6 13.♕h5+ ♔e7 14.♕f7+ ♔d6 15.♗f4+ (15.♘e4+ is weaker: 15...♗xe4 16.♗xe4) 15... e5 16.♗xb7 ♘xb7 17.♗xe5+ ♗xe5 18.♕g6+ ♕f6 19.♘e4+. Surprise!

11...♘c6 12.e5

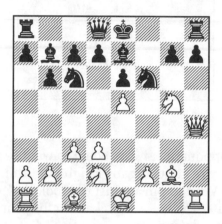

12...♘xe5

Giving up a piece, thus acquiescing to defeat.

12...♘d5 looks like the only move, but it offers no relief: 13.♘de4 ♘xe5 14.♕g3 ♘f7 15.♖xh7 ♖xh7 16.♘xh7 ♗f6 17.♘exf6+ gxf6 18.♗xd5 ♗xd5 19.♕g6+−.

13.♗xb7 ♘xd3+ 14.♔e2 ♘xc1+ 15.♖axc1 ♖b8 16.♗e4 ♕c8

17.♗g6+

Simple, but nice.

17...hxg6

17...♔f8 18.♖cg1 h6 19.♘f7 ♖g8 20.♕f4 d6 21.♘xh6 gxh6 22.♕xh6+ ♖g7 23.♗h5+−.

18.♕xh8+ ♗f8 19.♖h7

19.♘h7 ♔f7 20.♘xf6 ♔xf6 21.♖cg1 ♔e7 22.♕h4+ ♔d6 23.♖xg6+−. White wins more quickly in this line, but the move actually played is more spectacular!

19...♔e7 20.♖xg7+ ♔d6

20...♗xg7 (this capture also loses quickly) 21.♕xg7+ ♔d6 22.♕xf6 ♔c6 23.♕f3+ d5 24.c4+−:

21.♖f7 ♘d5 22.♕h2+ ♔c6 23.♔d1 ♗e7 24.♕g2 ♔d6 25.♘ge4+

In this kind of position featuring a king hunt, the mate is usually not too hard to find.

25...♔e5 26.♘c4#

74. KinoLeif – Nintedzhov

8 December 2016

1.c3 e5 2.d3 f5 3.♘d2 ♘f6 4.h3 d5

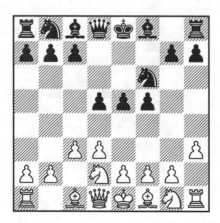

This game was submitted by a fan inspired by our previous book, *The Elshad System*.

5.♕c2

While this may not be White's best move, it does feature what we might call a certain "provocative temporizing." So Black decides to squash White completely.

5...c5 6.g4

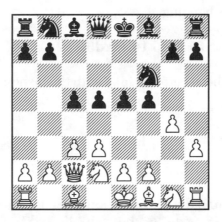

Here is the idea behind the Elshad Opening, in full flower – and precisely after the move ...c7-c5. Why so? Because we're bringing our light-squared bishop out to g2, from where it will exert pressure on the long diagonal. The d5-pawn is vulnerable because it can no longer be defended by its colleague from c6.

6...fxg4 7.hxg4 ♗xg4 8.♗g2 ♘c6 9.♘f1 ♖c8 10.♗g5 ♗e7 11.♘e3

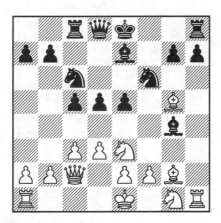

Just so! Black would rather not give up his light-squared bishop, so he will pull back.

11...♗e6 12.♕b3

The b-pawn is hanging.

12...♕d7 13.♗xf6 ♗xf6 14.♘xd5

It would have been better to take with the bishop on d5: 14.♗xd5! ♗xd5 15.♘xd5±.

14...♔f7 15.c4

And here Black lost... his Internet connection.

Stockfish 8 found the continuation 15.♘xf6. It's very strong and I recommend it: 15...gxf6 16.♗h3 ♗xb3 17.♗xd7.

1-0

---

75. Nemtsev_Igor (2879) – Goltzman_Evgeny (2546)

30 December 2015

1.c3 f5

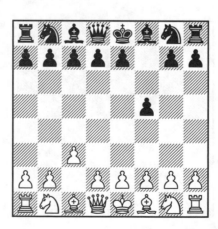

Evgeny Goltzman, a chess veteran from Saint Petersburg, fascinated me: whenever I would drop by Chess Planet, there he would be! After a day's hard work, if I decided to play in a night event, at

3 AM, he'd be there, too. We played a whole lot of games with each other; and although the score was heavily in my favor, I have to admit that sometimes he outplayed me. But when a player gets well past 70, of course, it gets difficult to move the mouse so quickly; so occasionally I would exploit this to save losing positions.

2.♕a4

I knew that Goltzman was in the habit of playing the Dutch, so I decided to employ a direct attack. The game turned out to be not wholly correct.

2...♘f6 3.h3 b6 4.g4

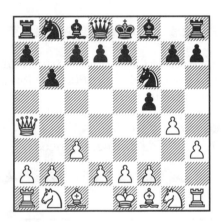

Arrogance, of course.

4...♗b7 5.♖h2

I had to – I couldn't play 5.f3?.

5...e6 6.d3 ♗d6 7.♗f4 e5 8.♗g5 h6 9.♗c1

Unconventional play always makes your opponent use up a lot of strength and time. It's one of the virtues of this opening.

9...e4 10.♖g2 exd3 11.gxf5

A completely deliberate exchange sacrifice. There will be another one later.

11...dxe2 12.♘xe2 ♗xg2 13.♔xg2 ♘c6 14.♕c4

Preventing Black from castling, for the time being at least. Here it's important not to give Black any solid guideposts, but to keep posing challenges for him to resolve.

14.♗xc6 dxc6 15.♕xc6+ ♔f8 16.♘d4 ♕e8+ 17.♘e6+ ♔f7 18.♕c4 b5 19.♕b3 ♔e7 20.♗e3 yields mutual chances.

14...♘e5 15.♕b3 c6 16.♗e3 ♘d3+ 17.♔f1 ♘c5 18.♕c4 b5 19.♕h4 ♕e7 20.♘d2 0-0-0

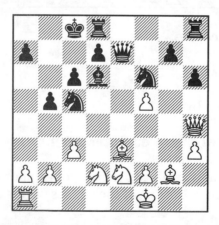

No big deal; I'll just shift my assault to the queenside.

21.a4 ♘xa4 22.♖xa4

As they say, this is not the time to relax. I've got to beat on the one spot with all I have. Naturally, the number of pieces left at the end doesn't count.

22...bxa4 23.♕xa4 ♗c5

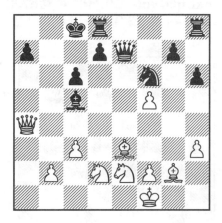

24.♘c4

Possibly not the most accurate: a queen check on a6 could have won right away. See the following variations: 24.♕a6+ ♔b8 (24... ♔c7 25.♗f4+ ♗d6 26.♕xa7+ ♔c8 27.♘c4 ♗xf4 28.♘b6# – a sweet little mate!) 25.♘b3 (I just want to grab the bishop) 25...♗xe3 26.♘a5 (threatens mate in one, so Black's reply is forced) 26...d5 27.♘xc6+ ♔c7 28.♘xe7.

24...♔b8 25.♘d4 ♖he8 26.♗xc6 ♗xd4 27.♕b5+

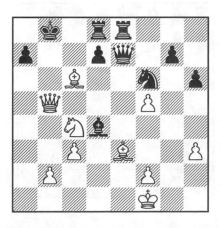

Leads to mate. There was another possibility, which would also be mate: 27.♗f4+. After this, everything is forced: 27...d6 28.cxd4 ♖d7 29.♗xd6+ ♖xd6 30.♕b4+ ♔c8 31.♘xd6+ ♔d8 32.♕b8#. A lovely sight!

27...♗b6 28.♘xb6 dxc6 29.♘d7+ ♔c7 30.♕a5+ ♔xd7 31.♕xa7+ ♔d6 32.♗f4+ ♔d5 33.♕d4#

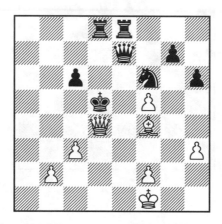

76. nemtsevguru (2341) – MrZor (2357)

lichess.org, 30 April 2016

1.c3 e6 2.♕a4 f5

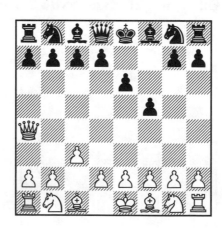

In this game, we see how a fan of the Dutch Defense handles Black. He plays it no matter what. But against the Elshad Opening, the Dutch Defense is a most welcome reply, since the f5-pawn is precisely the target we need for our customary g2-g4 push.

3.h3 ♘f6 4.g4 fxg4

Although this capture is natural enough, it's still weak because it opens the h-file. For the time being, this does not bother Black – he just doesn't realize where the blow is coming from.

5.♗g2 gxh3

But this is pure greed. Black doesn't see why he shouldn't take on h3.

6.♘xh3

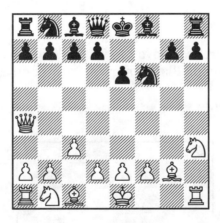

One of the "main lines" in this variation. If Black now castles short, then he will almost certainly be mated on either the g- or the h-file. Now he notices this and prepares to evacuate the king to the queenside.

6...♘c6 7.d3 d5 8.♘d2 ♗d7 9.♘f1

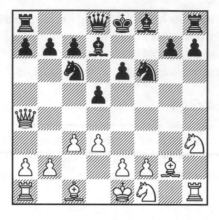

An important revelation for a lot of my opponents. They thought they were threatening my queen by the c6-knight's potentially jumping away. The fact is that Black has no useful discovery with his knight. Meanwhile, the clock keeps ticking while he searches for one.

9...♕e7 10.♘g5

One more theoretical move. On g5, this knight looms over Black's kingside and grates on Black's nerves. So, of course, he drives it off.

10...h6 11.♘g3

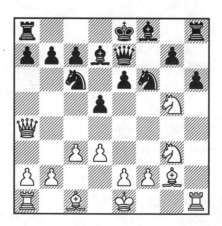

Oops! It turns out that the knight isn't going anywhere, on account of the pin on the rook.

11...0-0-0 12.♗e3 e5 13.c4

Opening the last few doors in front of Black's king. I have carried out more than a few such attacks; and this is a typical construction. Study it, and remember.

13...dxc4 14.dxc4 ♞d4 15.♕xa7

Threatening mate on the move.

15...♗c6 16.♗h3+

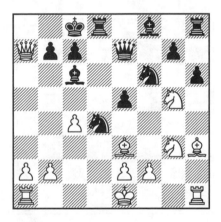

And here is our finishing touch. Now Black is forced to block his king's escape square, upon which there follows checkmate.

16...♖d7

After making this move with practically no time left, my opponent resigned.

1-0

Chapter 6

//

Black Has No Idea What to Do: Miscellaneous Replies

77. NemtsevIgor (2218) – sion2200 (2170)

Live Chess Chess.com, 13 June 2016

1.d3 c5 2.c3 g6 3.♕a4 ♗g7 4.g4 ♘c6 5.♗g2 h5

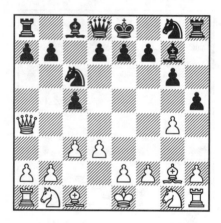

An oft-seen reaction from Black. There is an idea behind it. Here, I have played both g-pawn moves.

6.gxh5

Or 6.g5. Both moves are quite good; it's a matter of taste.

6...♖xh5 7.♘d2 d5 8.♘f1 ♘f6 9.♘g3 ♖h8 10.h4

Black's problem is that he can no longer castle kingside; and as a rule, the majority of chessplayers know, and consider it correct, to somehow remove their kings from the center. Which means most likely that Black will seek to castle queenside here.

10...♗d7 11.♘f3 ♛c7 12.♘g5 0-0-0 13.♗f4?

13.♘xf7 was of course much stronger. This was, after all, the idea behind bringing this knight to g5: to zero in on f7. In my defense, I must say that this was three-minute blitz, and we sometimes make moves there that we had not intended. In no way did I expect that my opponent would simply blunder.

13...e5 14.♗e3 d4 15.♗d2 ♖df8

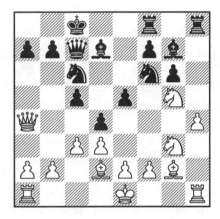

16.♛b3

16.cxd4!?. Elshad practically never plays this, believing that the c3-pawn should stay put. But in this concrete position, capturing would have been stronger: 16...exd4 17.♖c1 ♚b8 18.♖xc5±.

16...♗g4 17.f3

We see this move many times in this book. Unfortunately for Black, he has no way of exploiting the position of my knight on g3.

17...♗h5

17...e4 18.♘3xe4±.

18.♘3e4 ♘xe4 19.♘xe4 b6

20.a4

A standard way of moving the attack forward, attempting to pry open the a-file. Another way is 20.♕b5!? f5 21.♘g5 (threatening ♘e6) 21...♖e8 22.♖g1 (waiting in ambush; we are also looking at the g6-pawn) 22...dxc3 23.bxc3 ♔b8, with chances for both sides.

In this kind of position, if you're playing blitz, by this time your opponent's flag is falling. What's he going to play here? I don't know: there's no break with ...e5-e4. As for us – with White, we're going to play the a2-a4-a5 ram, and somewhere along the line we'll play e2-e3 to open up our fianchettoed bishop.

20...♗h6 21.♗xh6 ♖xh6 22.a5 ♘xa5 23.♕a4 ♖fh8 24.♔d2

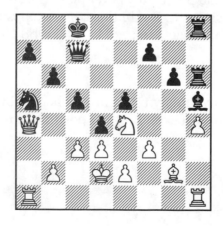

I've seen Elshad play this move many times. The rooks are now connected, while the king is placed excellently on d2. But there was a somewhat better alternative in 24.b4!±. A direct assault! Here it is: 24...♘b7 (24...cxb4 25.cxb4 ♘c6 26.♖c1 ♔b7 27.b5 ♘a5 28.♖xc7+) 25.♕xa7.

24...dxc3+ 25.bxc3 f5 26.♘g3 e4 27.♘xh5 ♖xh5 28.fxe4 ♖xh4 29.♖xh4 ♖xh4 30.♕e8+ ♕d8 31.♕xg6 fxe4 32.♖f1+−

Throwing the inactive rook into the offensive. Curiously, Black's king is less well protected than White's. Even *Stockfish* agrees with this, giving an evaluation of +3.62.

32...exd3 33.exd3 ♘c4+ 34.♔c1 ♘d6 35.♖f6 ♕e7 36.♖e6 ♖h6 37.♕xh6 ♘f7 38.♖xe7 ♘xh6 39.♖h7 1-0

78. Nemtsev – Salov S.

Sokolniki Rapid, 12 June 2015

1.d3 g6 2.c3 ♗g7

(see diagram next page)

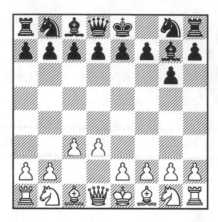

This game was played over the board in a rapid tournament (10 minutes per side, plus 5 seconds per move) against an experienced IM, who was twice the World Individual Champion of what is now the International Chess Committee of the Deaf.

Regarding the position: when Black fianchettoes his bishop, for some time he considers it protected. Let's think a little bit about the fianchetto employed in the Elshad. White doesn't ever intend to play d3-d4. Consequently, the g7-bishop already looks rather useless, crashing against White's c3-pawn. But the worst is yet to come. The g6-pawn is now clearly a target for White's h-pawn. Thus, I cannot recommend playing a fianchetto against the Elshad.

3.♕a4

This only looks like a premature development of the queen, as the classical school of chess would teach us. This is how they thought about the Réti Opening, the Grünfeld Defense, the Sokolsky Opening, and the Grob; and about the Elshad Opening, too. The queen doesn't go there just to stay there, it goes there in order to reach the h4 square. In this game, you will learn of still another twist on this queen transfer. All of this is quite unusual; and our opponents spend much time and rage trying to refute this opening.

3...c5 4.g4

At once! We do this in order to frighten the black knight and deter it from coming out to f6.

4...♘c6 5.♗g2 a6

5...d6.

6.♘d2 b5

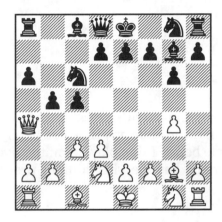

7.♕f4

Here comes the switch. We need the queen on the kingside.

7...♗b7 8.♘gf3 d6 9.h4 e5 10.♕g3 h5

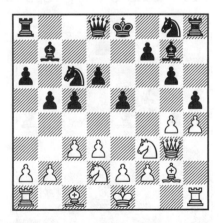

A rather concrete decision, leaving the black king uncastled for now. In the Elshad System, White doesn't even plan to castle, because the idea is, among other things, to control the center from the flanks; and from a psychological angle, to keep our opponents waiting to see which way we are going to castle.

In this case, we could have also played g4-g5.

11.gxh5

11.g5.

11...♖xh5 12.♘g5

At this point, my opponent's clock had already run from 10 minutes down to 3; meanwhile, my time had barely started ticking down. For the time being, I was playing on the five extra seconds per move. This wreaks havoc on his thinking process.

12...♘f6

12...♕f6.

12...♕e7 13.♗f3 ♖h8 14.h5 gxh5 15.♖xh5 (15.♗xh5) 15...♖xh5 16.♗xh5 ♘h6 – this variation was more or less acceptable for Black.

13.♘de4 ♘xe4 14.♗xe4 ♕f6 15.♕g2 ♖c8 16.♗d5 ♖c7

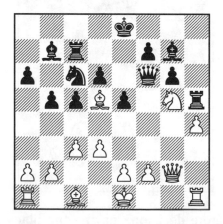

17.a4

17.♘xf7! would have been strong and beautiful; I didn't see it. Check out the variations: they look very convincing to me. On the other hand, the actual game variation looks pretty amazing, too.

After 17.♘xf7, there could follow 17...♖xf7 18.♗g5 (18.♗xc6+ ♗xc6 19.♕xc6+ ♔f8 20.♕a8+ ♔e7 21.♗g5 ♖xg5 22.♕b7+ ♔f8 23.♕c8+ ♔e7 24.hxg5 ♕xf2+ 25.♔d2 ♕f4+ 26.♔c2 ♕e3 27.♖ae1+−) 18... ♕xf2+ 19.♕xf2 ♖xf2 20.♔xf2 ♘a5 21.♗xb7 ♘xb7+−.

17...♘d8 18.♗e3 ♗xd5 19.♕xd5 b4

Else I would have played a4xb5, opening the file for my rook.

20.♘e4 ♕e6 21.♘xd6+ ♔d7

Or 21...♔f8 22.♕xe6 ♘xe6 23.♘e4.

22.♕xe6+ ♔xe6 23.♘e8 1-0

Black resigned, as he must lose material.

This was a tournament dedicated to Russia Day *[national holiday commemorating the independence of the Russian Federation from the Soviet Union – Ed.]*. There were several grandmasters and international masters among the one hundred or so participants. I came too late for the first couple of rounds, but then scored 6½ in the last 7 rounds and shared 2nd-6th places. And in all seven of these games, I used the Elshad System with both White and Black. Unfortunately, I could not reconstruct the rest of my games here.

79. Nemtsev_Igor (2844) – Bezdarnyi (2423)

1 June 2016

1.c3 ♘c6 2.♕a4 d6 3.g4 a6

Pretty dogmatic. Black probably wishes to drive off my queen with ...b7-b5.

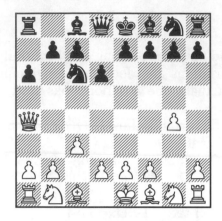

4.h3

A standard solution. I advise you to try out these other two moves in practice:

1) 4.♗g2. No fear, since the bishop's presence on the long diagonal clearly outweighs the loss of the g-pawn; and

2) 4.g5. A very interesting possibility which scatters my opponent's dominoes: he cannot bring out his knight normally to f6 now. And, on the whole, this game clearly shows how, even if he can stave off White's attack for the game's 3 minutes, he will simply lose on time, so complex will be the problems that I pose.

4...e5 5.♗g2 ♗d7 6.d3

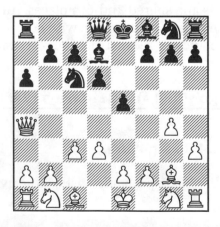

This usually comes as a big surprise for my opponent. For it looks like his bishop is threatening my queen, and so the queen "must" retreat. But the truth is that the knight has no good sideways leap; so he looks for one while his clock ticks away, and his sense of frustration grows at not being able to refute White's play.

6...♘ge7 7.♘d2 g6 8.♘f1

8.♘e4!? ♗g7 9.♗g5 is an interesting try: I would recommend it.

8...♗g7 9.♘g3 0-0 10.g5

With this move, it's as though White had now pressed the pawns of Black's castled position down into their squares.

10...f5?

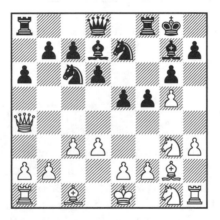

11.gxf6 *e.p.*

As a rule, taking *en passant* has to be done immediately.

11...♗xf6 12.h4 ♘f5

It's as though, in such positions, it seems to Black that it is he who is attacking White's uncastled king.

13.♘e4 ♗g7 14.♘f3

14.♕b3+ (an excellent move, which unfortunately I did not play) 14...♔h8 15.h5 gxh5 16.♖xh5±.

14...h6 15.h5 g5 16.♘fxg5! hxg5 17.h6

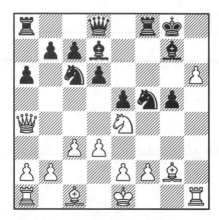

17.♕b3+!. Another oversight. Again, the queen check was stronger than the text: 17...♔h8 18.♗xg5 ♘ce7 19.h6+−.

17...♗xh6 18.♗h3

18.♖xh6 − I didn't see this excellent move. White's attack may run into a dead end, but the game itself, the non-standard problems that I would be setting for my opponent, would be what did the trick. Here he had mere seconds left on his clock − maybe 20-30 seconds until his flag fell. It was no longer of any relevance that I would be a rook down. Really, when you're playing blitz, you can't win here. After 18...♘xh6 19.♗xg5 ♘e7 20.♕b3+ ♔g7 21.0-0-0, White's attack continues.

18...♔g7 19.♗xf5 ♖xf5 20.♘g3 ♕e7 21.♕e4 ♖af8 22.♗e3 ♗e6 23.♔d2

Of course I'm not taking the rook. When your opponent's flag is hanging, all you need is to make simple moves and not allow him to trade pieces.

23...d5 24.♕g2 d4 25.♘h5+ ♔g6 26.♕h3 ♖h8 27.♘g3 dxe3+ 28.fxe3 ♖ff8 29.♕h5+ ♔g7 30.♘e4 ♕f7 31.♕h2 ♕g6 32.♖ag1 ♗d5 33.♖g4 ♗xe4 34.♖xe4 ♖f5 35.b4 ♖hf8 36.♕h3 b5 37.♖h2 ♖8f7 38.♕g3 ♕e6 39.c4 bxc4 40.♖xc4 e4 41. ♕xg5+

"Move-trolling" at the game's close. Black has one second left, so I have to make a move that he'd never expect: I give my queen away. It's a typical trick in Internet blitz.

1-0

80. Nemtsev_Igor (2838) – OlegA (2630)

14 May 2017

1.c3 g6 2.♕a4 ♗g7 3.g4 h5

A technique I've met often, which indicates that my opponent is a good player. He is familiar with this strategic idea.

4.g5

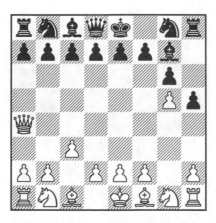

In addition to this move, I have also played the straightforward capture. There are other games like that in this book.

4...h4

Original, but nothing more than that. The stray h-pawn will soon succumb.

5.♘f3 c6 6.♘xh4 d5 7.♘f3 e5 8.d3 ♘d7 9.h4 ♘e7 10. ♘bd2 ♘f5 11.♗g2 ♘b6 12.♕c2 ♗e6 13.e4

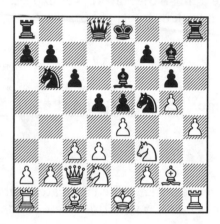

With a black knight on f5, bringing the white knight to g3 or e3 no longer works.

13...dxe4 14.♘xe4 ♘d6 15.♘f6+

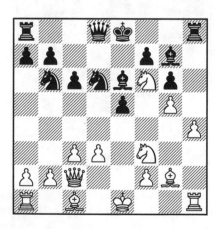

A natural pawn sacrifice, in return for which White gets full compensation. All the action will take place on Black's increasingly weak dark squares.

15...♗xf6 16.gxf6 ♕xf6 17.♗g5 ♕f5 18.♕e2

White threatens ♗h3.

18...e4 19.♘d4 ♕d5 20.dxe4 ♕c4 21.♘xe6 ♕xe6 22.b3 f6 23.♗f4 0-0-0 24.♗h3 f5 25.exf5 ♕xe2+ 26.♔xe2 ♘xf5 27. ♗g5

This is good, but there was a stronger continuation: 27.♗xf5! gxf5 28.c4, seizing the d5 square from Black's pieces – principally the knight. The passed h-pawn is decisive.

27...♖de8+ 28.♔f1 ♔c7 29.♗g4 ♘d5 30.c4 ♘c3 31.♗f6

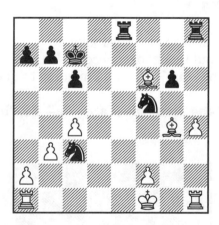

Again, 31.♗xf5 would have been much stronger: 31...gxf5 32.♗f6 ♘e4 33.♗xh8 ♖xh8 34.h5+−.

31...♘e3+

This gives Black some kind of chance; I overlooked this move.

32.fxe3 ♖hf8 33.♔g2 ♖xf6 34.♖ae1 ♘e4 35.♖hf1 ♖d6 36.♖e2 ♖h8 37.♖f7+ ♔b6 38.♗f3 ♘c3 39.♖c2

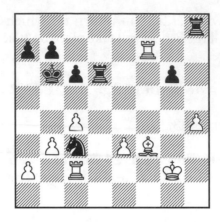

Suddenly we see that the black knight cannot leave c3 because of c4-c5+.

39...♖xh4 40.♖xc3 ♖d2+ 41.♔g3 ♖hh2 42.c5+ ♔a6 43.♔f4 ♖xa2 44.b4 ♖hb2 45.♗e4 ♖xb4 46.♔f3 ♖aa4 47. ♗d3+ ♔a5 48.♖f4

Truth be told, I had given away too many pawns, and in a piece-up ending, you should exchange pieces. It's a good thing I still have my e-pawn, because that's the one I'm going to queen.

48...g5 49.♖xb4 ♖xb4 50.♖a3+ ♖a4 51.♖b3 ♖b4 52.♖c3 ♔a4 53.e4

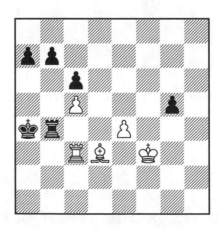

53...♖b3

It goes without saying that many moves win here: we are playing three-minute blitz, with no increment. After a certain point, games proceed in rapid-fire fashion: you just make your intended moves, one after the other.

54.♖c4+ ♔a3 55.♔e3 g4 56.e5 g3 57.♖g4 g2 58.♖xg2 ♔b4 59.♖g4+ ♔xc5 60.♖d4 1-0

81. Elshad – Dragomaretsky

6 May 2015

1.c3 c5 2.♕a4 ♘c6 3.g4 d5 4.♗g2 ♖b8

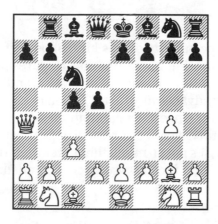

My good friend Evgeny Dragomaretsky is a very strong international master who has probably played a hundred thousand games in his lifetime. He literally lives and breathes chess! Nevertheless, in this game, he was unable to handle the novel positions that arose.

5.h3 b5

What's clear is that this was the idea behind Black's previous move. The Master simply doesn't know that the opposing queen is quite ready to travel across the chessboard without prodding.

6.♕c2

6.♕f4 e5 7.♕g3 was also possible, although riskier. On the other hand, this Elshad System isn't a very quiet opening, either.

6...e5 7.d3 ♗e6

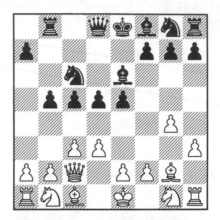

An important peculiarity of this kind of powerful occupation of the center is the fact that his center now requires piece protection. Consider: Black has four pawns, all in a row, standing on his fourth rank. If they don't advance any further, then in effect they will function as weaknesses, since they cannot defend one another. But if they do advance, then weak squares will appear behind them. Thus, as the classics say, it's not so much the center itself that's important, it's the possibility that it can be securely defended.

8.♘d2 ♕d7 9.a4

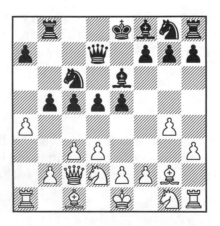

The first break. He really would rather not defend his b-pawn with ...a7-a6, because after axb5 axb5, the a-file falls into White's hands.

9...b4 10.a5!

Freeing the a4 square for the white queen. The wind is starting to whistle around Black's queenside light squares.

10...&d6 11.&gf3

Threatening 12.&g5.

11...f6 12.&a4 &ge7 13.&h4 &g6 14.&f5 0-0

14...&xf5 15.gxf5 &xf5?? 16.&xc6+.

15.&f1 &fc8 16.&1g3 &f8 17.h4

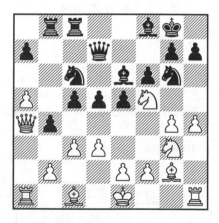

Launching the attack. One of the chief features of the position is that White is executing a flank attack, to which Black should reply with a counterstrike in the center. But there is no center, and therefore no central confrontation – nothing for Black to latch onto.

17...bxc3 18.bxc3 d4 19.h5 &f4

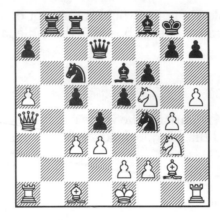

A critical position. White finds a non-standard solution: exchanging his powerful bishop. The point is that it's less important which pieces are traded off than which ones *remain* on the board, because in this position it's the knights which are left with superb support points in the center.

20.♗xc6 ♕xc6 21.♕xc6 ♖xc6 22.c4

White is careful to keep the queenside closed.

22...g6 23.hxg6 hxg6 24.♘h6+ ♗xh6 25.♖xh6 ♔g7 26.g5 fxg5 27.♖h2 ♗f5 28.♔d1 g4 29.♔c2 a6 30.♗d2 ♖cc8 31.♖hh1 ♖h8 32.♖hb1 ♔f6 33.♖b6+ ♖xb6 34.axb6 ♗c8 35.♘e4+

The famous Elshad knight!

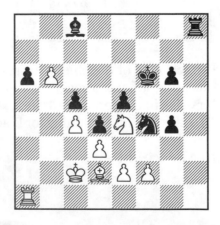

35...♔e7 36.♘xc5 ♗d7 37.♗b4 ♗c6 38.♖xa6 ♘e6 39.b7 1-0

82. Elshad – Semenov

May 2000

1.c3 c5 2.♕a4 ♘c6 3.d3 d5 4.h3 e5 5.g4 f5

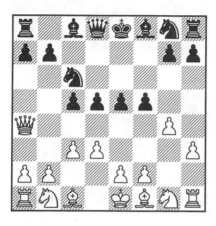

A penetrating blow – at least, that's what Black must be thinking. For those in the know about the Elshad I say that now, on the board, we have the Elshad Opening in its purest form. If you read my book on the Elshad for Black, then you will see that this position is exactly like one of those in that book, but with colors reversed and therefore an extra tempo for White.

6.♗g2 fxg4 7.♘d2

This version of the System grants Black a little "hiccup": ...g4-g3. 7.hxg4 is better (7...♗xg4? 8.♕xg4).

7...♘f6 8.♘f1 ♕c7 9.♘g3 gxh3 10.♘xh3

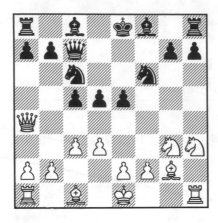

Just so! Now the knight will lead the way to g5. Meanwhile, ...h7-h6 will pose no inconvenience.

10...b6

10...h6 11.♘g5.

11.♘g5 ♗d7 12.♗h3 ♗xh3 13.♖xh3 ♕d7 14.♖b1 ♗e7 15.f3 h6 16.♘f5 0-0

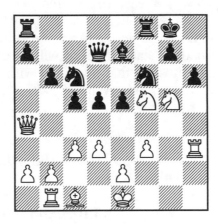

Still, Black castles. White's next move cries out to be played. At any rate, a formulaic approach to the game would always show that the black king is castled, while White's is "stranded in the center."

16...♕xf5 17.♕xc6+ would be horrible.

17.♘xh6+ gxh6 18.♖xh6 ♔g7 19.♕h4 ♖h8 20.♘e6+ ♕xe6 21.♕g5+ ♔f7 22.♕g6+ ♔f8 23.♖xh8+ ♘g8 24.♗h6#

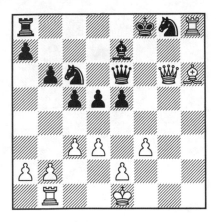

The whole attack was carried out in s single breath. All of the last few moves were practically forced.

83. Elshad – NN

1.c3 ♘f6 2.♕a4 c5 3.g4 ♘c6 4.b4

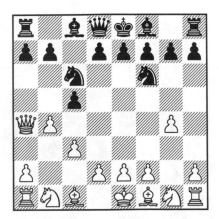

Here we see the unbelievable depth of Elshad's thinking. He conducted this game against a player whose name is unknown to us. Elshad himself explained his idea thus: this is an occupation of the center from the flanks. True, after a very short while, the game takes on "book" contours.

4...cxb4 5.cxb4 g6 6.d3 ♗g7 7.♗g2 0-0 8.♘c3 d6 9.b5 ♘a5 10.g5 ♘e8 11.♗d2

What's clever about this is that Black should not defend the knight at once against the X-ray near-threat of White's d2-bishop by playing ...b7-b6, as then his a8-rook hangs.

White can also start his attack on Black's king directly: 11.h4 ♖b8. Now 12.♗a3?? doesn't work because the c3-knight hangs to 12...♗xc3+ (if 12...b6, then 13.♖c1).

11...♖b8 12.h4 b6 13.♖c1 ♗d7 14.h5 a6 15.♕h4

This sort of position comes up a lot in this book – one of the *tabiyas* of the opening.

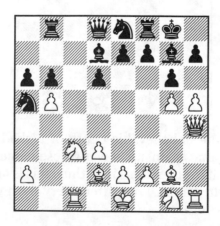

15...gxh5 16.♗e4 f5 17.♗f3

Mate is forced once the bishop joins the attack on h5.

1-0

84. Papin, V. – Rubanov

1.c3 c5 2.♕a4 ♘c6 3.♕h4

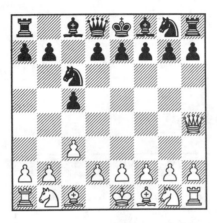

The future grandmaster Vasily Papin played White here. Elshad himself gave Vasya a few lessons when he was about ten years old. Transferring the queen now may be showing his cards too soon, but let's see...

3...♘f6 4.g4 e6 5.♗g2 ♗e7 6.g5 ♘d5 7.d3 h6

Black thinks that this pin favors him. However, after White's reply, it becomes clear that the first player looked a little more deeply into it...

8.♘f3 hxg5??

Yes, this was a blunder, but Black was "obligated" to blunder at some point, because this usually happens when somebody is meeting the Elshad Opening for the first time.

9.♕xh8+ ♝f8 10.♝xg5 1-0

85. Nemtsev_Igor (2887) – Markov_Vladimir (2829)

14 July 2017

1.c3 d6 2.♕a4+ ♝d7

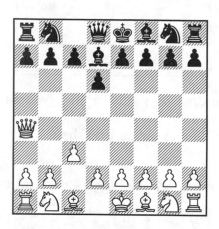

A natural reaction by Black to White's queen check.

3.♕b3

Closely examining the b7-pawn, but the main idea is to keep an eye on the a2-g8 diagonal.

3...♗c6 4.d3 e5 5.♘d2 f5 6.♘gf3

For now, 6.♕e6+? ♘e7 doesn't carry much force.

6...♘f6 7.h3

Avoiding the trap – although it's possible that Black hadn't even seen it: 7.♕e6+ ♗e7 8.♕xf5 ♗d7 9.♕g5 ♘g4 10.♕xg7 ♗f6, and the queen is trapped.

7...g6 8.g4 fxg4 9.hxg4 ♘xg4

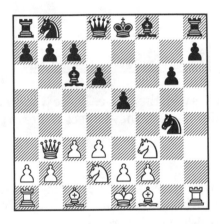

10.♗h3

White should now have taught Black what can happen when you recklessly take on g4: 10.♕e6+ ♕e7 11.♕c8+ ♕d8 12.♕xg4.

10...♘f6 11.♘f1 ♗g7 12.♗g5 ♘bd7 13.♘e3 ♕e7 14.a4 h6 15.♗h4 0-0-0 16.a5 a6 17.♖g1 g5 18.♗g3 ♘h5 19.♗g2 ♘f4 20.♗h1 ♘c5 21.♕c2 e4 22.dxe4 ♘xe4 23.♘d4 ♗xd4 24.cxd4 ♘xg3 25.♗xc6 bxc6 26.♖xg3 ♔d7 27.♖c1 c5 28.dxc5 d5 29. c6+ ♔e8 30.♘g4 h5 31.♖e3 ♘e6 32.♕g6+ ♔f8 33.♖xe6 hxg4 34.♖xe7 ♔xe7 35.♖c3 ♖d6 36.♖e3+ ♔d8 37.♕xg5+ ♔c8 38.♕xg4+ ♔b8 39.♖b3+ ♔a8 40.♕b4 1-0

86. Elshad – Azizyan

1.c3 c5

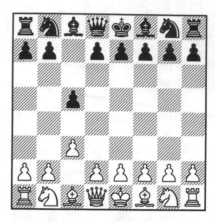

Black often replies with this move. Those who employ it are either Sicilian Defense devotees, or they expect White to play d2-d4 next.

2.♕a4

Zap! Well, what do we do now? Can't play ...d7-d5. No, we have to start using our own mind already on move 2. Yet another psychological edge for Elshad players.

2...♘f6 3.g4

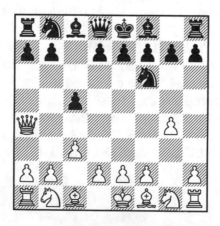

My head is spinning. What kind of feelings must Black be experiencing, seeing all of this? So White probably wants to continue g4-g5 ? Do we need to stop this by ...h7-h6 ?

3...♞c6

At the moment, Black does not consider that preventive move necessary.

4.d3

White is in no hurry either. This is the author's basic setup. Let Black worry constantly about the g4-g5 advance.

4...d6 5.h3

Black threatened to take the pawn on g4.

5...g6

This only looks safest. In reality, it is precisely the fianchetto that gets destroyed the worst in Elshad's Opening. Why? Simple: the g6-pawn becomes the clear focus of White's attack.

6.g5 ♞d5

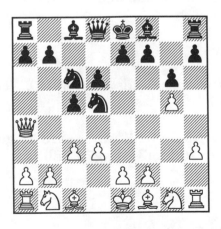

Of course we don't want to retreat to g8. Many do move out to h5, e.g. 6...♞h5 7.♗g2 ♗d7 8.♗f3. And that's the problem with it, it turns out. You should remember this maneuver for White.

7.h4 ♗g7

7...♞b6 8.♕f4 e5 9.♕h2 ♗g7 10.♗g2 0-0 11.h5. Still another way to bring the queen to the king's wing.

8.h5 0-0 9.♕h4

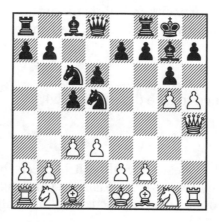

We have before us the whole idea behind this opening. Black has made all of his normal developing moves – and already he can resign.

9...gxh5 10.e4

10.♕xh5 (this move also leads to victory) 10...♖e8 11.♕xh7+ ♚f8 12.g6 fxg6 13.♗h6.

10...♞c7 11.♕xh5 ♖e8 12.♕xh7+ ♚f8 13.g6 fxg6 14.♗h6 ♞e6 15.♕xg6 ♞e5 16.♗xg7+ ♞xg7 17.♖h8#

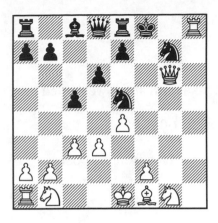

87. Elshad – Petrunia

1996

1.c3 ♘f6 2.♕a4 c5 3.g4 ♘c6 4.b4

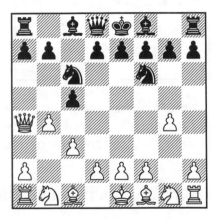

This kind of move would confuse anybody. The idea is to advance the pawn, pushing the knight off a good square.

4...cxb4

Not 4...♘xg4 5.b5.

5.cxb4 g6

Logical: Black takes aim at the weakened long diagonal.

6.♘c3 ♗g7 7.♗g2 0-0 8.b5

The first knight is driven from its post.

8...♘a5 9.g5

And now it's the other knight's turn. Note that the fourth rank has been cleared for the transfer of the white queen to the kingside. I'm sure that Black didn't understand any of this throughout the whole game.

9...♘e8 10.h4 ♖b8 11.♗a3 d6 12.♖c1 ♗d7 13.h5

Everything is going according to plan. Black sees he is under attack from the h-pawn. But, as a rule, the fact that the queen is also headed for that wing is something that players of Black understand only after it arrives there.

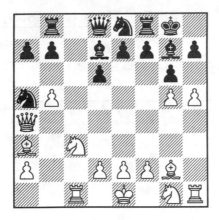

13...a6 14.♕h4

"Is everything all right?", asks the queen of Black's king.

14...gxh5 15.♗e4 f5 16.♗f3

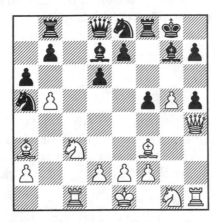

That's it! There is no defense against White's direct threat to capture everything on the h-file with his queen.

1-0

88. Nemtsev_Igor (2817) – NoCrazy (2839)

4 May 2017

1.c3 g6 2.♕a4 ♗g7 3.g4 c5 4.♗g2 ♘c6

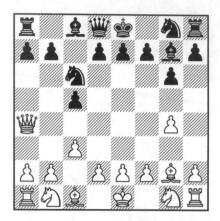

This is actually a "book" position in the Elshad Opening. When Black prepares to fianchetto the bishop, already it is 99% clear that he intends to castle short. So we can adopt a straightforward plan.

5.g5 h6

Instead of Black's playing ...h7-h6 and White's pushing his g-pawn to meet the black h-pawn, here Black nudges his pawn forward in reply to White's advance. White can reply in a number of ways. I decided to try the line in which the rooks are traded off on the h-file.

6.h4 hxg5 7.hxg5 ♖xh1 8.♗xh1 ♕c7

The black queen is angling for h2, so I have to hold it off.

9.♕h4 b5 10.d3 ♗b7 11.♗f4 ♘e5

I believe this was an inaccuracy. In any event, I can't recommend that you voluntarily submit yourself to a pin.

12.♘f3 d6 13.♘xe5 dxe5 14.♗e3

The best place for this bishop. From here, it controls two important diagonals, whereas from g3 it does not look as though he could extract any real benefit from the pin against the pawn.

14...♗xh1 15.♕xh1 ♖c8 16.♘d2 b4

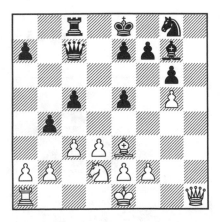

Strategically, things are already going downhill for Black. Look at the e4 square. White's knight (the Elshad knight) will be occupying an especially strong position there.

17.c4 e4 18.♘xe4 ♗xb2 19.♖d1 ♕e5 20.f4 ♕f5 21.♕f3 ♗d4 22.♗xd4 cxd4 23.♔d2 a5

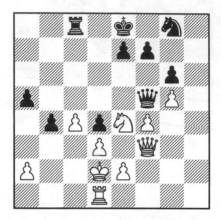

This is the right time to begin the attack on the opposing king. The rook moves over to the h-file in order to shoot up to the far end of the board.

24.♖h1 a4 25.♖h8 ♔f8 26.♘g3 ♕e6 27.f5 ♕e3+

Practically forced; keeping the queens on is more likely to result in Black's getting mated than in giving mate himself.

28.♕xe3 dxe3+ 29.♔xe3 b3 30.axb3 axb3 31.♔d2 ♖b8 32.♖h1 gxf5 33.♘xf5 e6 34.♘d4 ♘e7 35.♘b5 ♘f5 36.♖b1 ♔g7 37.♖xb3

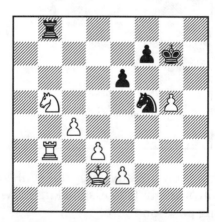

Black's passed pawn is gone; the rest is not complicated.

37...♚g6 38.e4 ♞g3 39.♚e3 ♖h8 40.♞d6 ♖h3 41.♚d4 ♞e2+ 42.♚c5 ♚xg5 43.♞xf7+ ♚f4 44.♖b7

Here my opponent ran out of time.

1-0

89. Nemtsev_Igor (2803) – GRIBABAS (2756)

4 May 2017

1.c3 c5 2.♕a4 g6

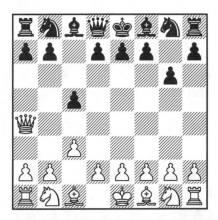

In strategic terms, this move looks like a mistake. Why? Think about it: the bishop will come out to g7, but White has already advanced his c-pawn to c3, which means that the bishop will be biting on granite.

3.h4

There's no need here to "follow theory" with h2-h3, g2-g4, etc.

3...♞f6 4.g4 a6 5.g5 b5

Consistent. Now I have to decide where to put my queen. Here, besides the text, I can also drop it back to c2, setting up an ambush...

6.♕f4 ♞h5 7.♕h2 e6 8.♗g2 d5 9.♗f3

A bit hasty: I should have played d2-d3 first, so that the black knight could not jump to f4.

9...♗d6 10.♕g2 ♘f4 11.♕f1 h5

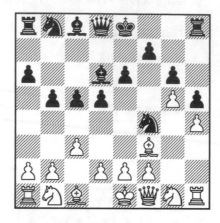

12.e3

On the other hand, the knight does drop.

12...♗b7 13.exf4 ♗xf4 14.♘e2 ♗c7 15.d4 c4 16.a4

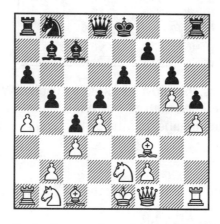

Now I have to find where to break into Black's position.

16...bxa4 17.♗f4 ♘c6 18.♕g2 ♘a5 19.♖xa4 ♘b3 20.♕g3 ♗xf4 21.♕xf4 0-0 22.♘d2 ♘xd2 23.♔xd2

Piece trades, as we know, favor the side that is ahead in material.

23...♗c6 24.♖a2 f5

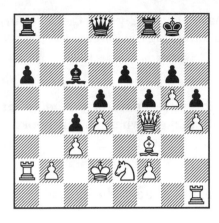

25.gxf6 *e.p.*

In most situations, you have to capture *en passant*. Here too, you must open up lines.

25...♖xf6 26.♕g3 ♕f8 27.♗xh5 ♔h7 28.♗g4 ♖xf2 29.h5 g5 30.h6 ♕f6 31.♕e3 ♗d7 32.♖h5 ♖f1 33.♖xg5 ♕xh6 34.♖h5 1-0

90. Papin – Lovkov

1999

1.c3 c5 2.♕a4 ♘c6 3.g4 ♘f6 4.♗g2 e6 5.g5

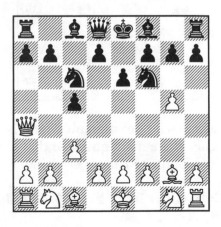

All right! We have played g2-g4 for the very purpose of pushing that pawn up and harassing the knight.

5...♘g8

I wouldn't call this retreat natural: 5...♘d5 was totally playable: we have games with that elsewhere in this book.

6.h4 d5 7.d3

Opening the knight's route to the kingside.

7...♗d6 8.♘d2 ♘ge7 9.♘f1 ♖b8

On the whole, this is just normal caution: for a long time, Black avoids castling short, as he understands the risks. On the other hand, it's obvious that, with his setup of pieces and pawns in the center, there will be no place to put his king.

10.h5 b5 11.♕h4

Good timing! For Black to castle now would be just awful. But what can he do? This is the main question that haunts everybody the first time they encounter Elshad's Opening.

11...b4 12.♘f3 bxc3 13.bxc3 ♕a5 14.♗d2 ♕a3 15.♘e3

It's important to note that Black has no pawn breaks in the center. If he moves any of his pawns to the fourth rank, then we'll take that pawn off immediately. This rule works wonders.

15...e5 16.h6 g6 17.0-0

Quite logical in this situation. Black's dark-square holes are enough of a factor to allow White not to have to risk leaving his king in the center any longer.

17...♗e6 18.♘g4 ♗xg4 19.♕xg4 0-0

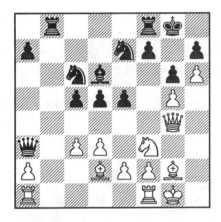

The future GM finds a way to get his queen to f6.

20.♘h4 ♕a6 21.♕f3 f5 22.gxf6

A required capture in order to open up the black king.

22...e4 23.dxe4 ♘e5 24.♕h3 ♘c8 25.♕e6+ 1-0

91. Elshad – NN

1997

1.c3 c5 2.♕a4 ♘c6 3.g4 ♘f6 4.b4

We have already seen this position. Elshad played many games in park settings, most of them in Sokolniki Park. It wasn't always possible to recall his opponents' names. The games were reconstructed out of our analyses together. This was one of these games.

4...cxb4 5.cxb4 g6 6.♘c3 ♗g7 7.♗g2 0-0 8.b5 ♘a5 9.g5 ♘e8 10.h4 ♖b8

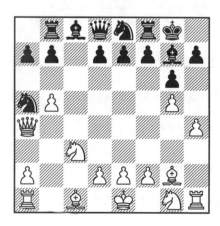

For us, the interest lies in how the attacking scheme is constructed.

11.h5

Freeing up h4 in preparation for shuttling the queen to that square. Black is blissfully unaware of this, especially considering that he is encountering this opening for the first time.

11...b6 12.♕h4 f6

Apparently, this creates *Luft* for Black's king.

13.hxg6 hxg6 14.♗e4

White's threat of the bishop capture, with mate to follow, forces Black to make his next move.

14...f5 15.♕h7+ ♔f7 16.♗xf5 gxf5 17.♕xf5+ ♔g8 18.♕h7+ ♔f7 19.g6+ ♔e6 20.♕h3+ ♔d6 21.♗a3+

We know that the king cannot survive like this; you can read it in any classic chess manual.

21...♔c7 22.♘d5+ ♔b7 23.♗xe7

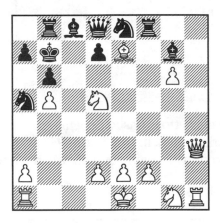

Only here it's the queen that dies. **1-0**

Two More Games by Elshad

1. Elshad Mamedov – Andrei Minsky

This game was played in a blitz tournament against a well-known FIDE Master. He wasn't unaware of the Elshad; he had played several games against this opening. Let's watch:

1.c3 ♘f6 2.♕a4 g6

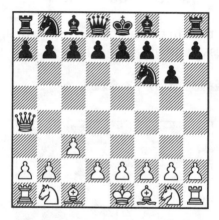

Choosing the fianchetto is based on a false sense of security in his short-castled position when, in fact, it is precisely the fianchetto pawn that frequently becomes the main point on which White fixes his attack.

3.d3 ♗g7 4.g4

As I have already written more than once, there's no sense in White's proceeding slowly with h2-h3 and then g2-g4.

4...c6

Blunting the action of White's light-squared bishop on g2.

5.g5

Immediately inquiring what the black knight's intentions are.

5...♘d5

This makes sense: on h5, it could come under attack from the bishop after ♗g2-f3.

6.h4

Clearly aiming at the bulge in Black's kingside formation.

6...♘b6 7.♕f4

The latest fashion in this variation. I, too, use this move, along with the retreat to c2.

7...e5

7...d5.

8.♕g3 d5

Black definitely likes what he's doing. The center is occupied, and now all that's left is to finish White off.

9.h5 ♕e7 10.♘f3

White's threats should not be underestimated. For example, after 11.h6, the e-pawn would be lost.

10...e4 11.h6

A hugely important in-between move, so as not to let the bishop out to e5.

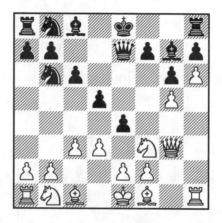

11...♗xc3+ 12.♘xc3 exf3 13.♗f4

Black wasn't expecting this. The problem for our opponents is that they're not taking into account that a completely unconventional opening is being played, so at every move, they expect something "normal" while a torpedo is headed straight for them.

13...♘a6

13...♘8d7 14.♗d6 ♕d8.

14.♗d6

Now Black definitely feels the loss of his dark-squared bishop.

14...♕e6

Else 15.♕e5+.

15.♗h3 f5 16.gxf6 *e.p.* ♕xf6 17.♗e5 ♕f8 18.♗g7

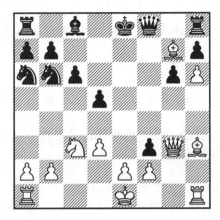

The master resigned here. A most impressive crush!

1-0

2. Elshad Mamedov – Valery Grechikhin

19 September 2017

1.c3 f5

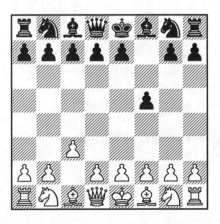

This game meant a lot to Elshad: it was played in the classic Aeroflot Open. Grandmaster Mikhail Golubev, in his tournament survey article on the "ChessPro" site, rated this game highly for its originality.

2.h3 ♘f6 3.g4 fxg4

"Of course," thinks Black, "why shouldn't I take it?"

4.hxg4 ♘xg4 5.♕a4

There is another possibility in this position, which Elshad has also used more than once: 5.♕c2 ♘f6. It looks like Black has to retreat his knight... but then, like thunder from a clear sky, there comes 6.♖xh7 ♖xh7 7.♕g6#.

5...♘f6 6.d3 c6 7.♘d2 e5 8.♘df3

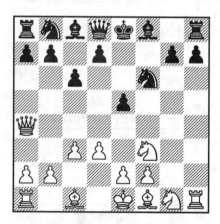

Quite sensible. The "standard" solution here is 8.♗g2, and then the knight on d2 goes to f1. But, since Black has already shown his cards by playing ...c7-c6 (with the idea of ...d7-d5), there is no reason for us to play along with ♗f1-g2.

8...♕e7 9.♗h3 e4 10.dxe4 ♕xe4

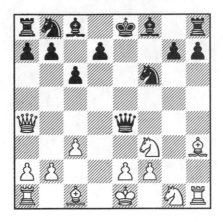

A very important novelty. It seems reasonable to attack with the queens on and so one would think that now we need to protect our queen from trades. But it turns out that it's also possible to simply exchange queens!

11.♕xe4+ ♘xe4 12.♗f5 ♘f6

Where else to go?

13.e4 ♔d8

In order to play ...d7-d5, which he can't do right now, because then White would just take the c8-bishop.

14.♘g5

Threatening ♘f7.

14...♔c7 15.e5 g6

If Black's knight moves, then ♘f7 followed by ♗xh7, and the g8-rook is toast, e.g. 15...♘d5 16.♘f7 ♖g8 17.♗xh7.

16.♗xg6 ♘g4 17.♗f4

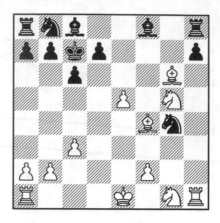

Finis. I just have to ask: what are all of Black's pieces doing on the eighth rank?

1-0

About the Author

FIDE Master Igor Evgenievich Nemtsev studied at the Chelyabinsk State Institute of Physical Culture (Chess Division) and has worked as a trainer for 25 years. His students include numerous players of all strengths, among them dozens of Candidate Masters, four FIDE Masters, and one International Master. In 2000, he shared 1st-4th places in the qualifier for the Russian Championship in the city of Vyatskiye Polyany. He is currently providing chess training in person and over the Internet, and managing children's classes and training camps.

The author's website is nemtsevChess.com